**W9-CMS-776**

# HIDDEN WORLDS
## FRESH CLUES TO THE PAST

# HIDDEN WORLDS

## FRESH CLUES
## TO THE PAST

Did Columbus, Magellan and Piri Reis
know the Glareanus maps?

by
M. H. J. Th. van der Veer and P. Moerman

SOUVENIR PRESS

First British edition published 1974 by Souvenir Press Ltd,
95 Mortimer Street, London W1N 8HP
and simultaneously in Canada by
J. M Dent & Sons (Canada) Ltd,
Ontario, Canada

ISBN 0 285 62130 0

Printed in Great Britain by
Richard Clay (The Chaucer Press), Ltd,
Bungay, Suffolk

# Contents

6

7

# Acknowledgements

A large number of people and institutions were consulted in the preparation of this book, and we should like to thank in particular the following for their much-appreciated assistance: Dr Kemal Cig, Curator of the Topkapi Sarayi Museum Istanbul; the British Museum, Natural History, London; Dr Svat Soucek of Michigan University; Diane Harlé and Jacques Vandin, the Louvre Museum, Paris; the Ashmolean Museum, Oxford; Dr H. D. Schneider, Rijksmuseum of Antiquities, Leiden; the Hermitage Museum, Leningrad; Dr M. von Beckerath, the University Library, Bonn; the Museum of Ethnology, Rotterdam; M. Madlung, West German Embassy, The Hague; Professor G. H. R. von Koenigswald of the Senckenberg Institute, Frankfurt am Main; the Institute of Human Biology, Utrecht; and Emile Fradin, Glozèl Museum, Glozèl.

# Introduction

Through his discoveries and his researches, man has been able to explain the story of the creation and evolution of our planet and its inhabitants to a limited extent. But the picture is still far from complete. Many issues are explained inadequately or not at all. For example, there is still no acceptable explanation of the mysteries of birth, life and death, while the problems of how the planet came to be formed and how human beings actually arose on it remain shrouded in obscurity; neither the simultaneous flourishing of cultures around 3000 B.C., nor the discovery of America long before the time of Columbus, have been satisfactorily explained.

This book sets out in some detail a new theory about the simultaneous development of the great civilizations of the ancient world; and while it certainly does not claim to offer a cut-and-dried solution to the discovery of America, it does show, by carefully following the story of Columbus and using all the available evidence, how historians have come to accept what they consider to be *the* discovery of America—which in fact cannot possibly have been its real discovery!

By letting the facts speak for themselves—and these facts were largely supplied by Columbus himself—we hope to demonstrate the validity of our arguments to those who simply accept conventional views about the discovery of America, and to convince them both by cold reason and by historical evidence which can no longer be questioned: and in this we will rely a good deal on the "Glareanus" map, which we ourselves discovered, and which outlines South America more precisely than many other maps produced years later. It provides us with indisputable evidence, putting even the voyages of discovery carried out by Magellan during 1521 and 1522 in a completely different light: for South America is not shown as being joined to the Antarctic land mass, but as terminating in a clearly defined point with sea all round it!

We shall also deal with long-standing misconceptions—some of which have endured for centuries—concerning the maps and charts produced by Martin Waldseemüller, a man for whom we have great admiration but who was certainly not the creator of the "oldest and most complete map of South America"! We shall also have something to say about the Piri Reis map, bearing in mind the fact that although people often talk about the Reis *maps* a second one has yet to be found

We fully appreciate that once we have convinced you that Columbus did not discover, but merely re-discovered, America it becomes our responsibility to try to find out who really discovered it. Thor Heyerdahl has already demonstrated the feasibility of early voyages of discovery in boats made of papyrus, which had hitherto been considered too unreliable for the purpose but were in fact used by the early Egyptians before they succeeded in building completely sea-worthy wooden ships. Did the Egyptians discover America? Other clues can be found in ancient Egypt and indeed in all the old civilizations; one particular trail leads us back to the oldest civilization on earth, while another, which is supposed to have had its origin in the Dark Ages, runs back from Columbus to a great race of sea-farers whose splendid achievements have hitherto been unknown to us.

We have found numerous new clues and pieces of evidence which have yet to be investigated in detail but which lead to some inescapable conclusions, one of which is that long before the time of Columbus there must have been contact between Europe and the New World.

It is quite true that the civilizations of America had developed for a long time in isolation; yet the Spaniards who brought "civilization" to America found as soon as they disembarked that what they saw contained numerous affinities with civilization that had flourished in the Old World before the time of Christ! This provides more evidence of the discovery of America

12

before Columbus; other clues and similarities which support our case can be found in, for example, the architecture and in certain aspects of primitive religious ceremonies common to both the Old and the New Worlds.

We also examine the problems posed by the enigmatic megaliths, and by Glozel and Atlantis, subjects which seemed to crop up in totally unexpected places whenever we dealt with ancient civilizations and other subjects—a warning that we were not to imagine early civilizations as being separate from each other but rather as having undergone similar stages of development in several respects, even if they were not related originally. To hesitate about accepting this proposition would be rather the same as to agree with the arbitrary date which scientists have fixed at around 3000 B.C. to mark the development of the ancient civilizations; and it would be just as misleading to assume that people who lived before that date necessarily belonged to the Stone Age. History is not just a matter of drawing a line through a period in order to fit it into a preconceived theory.

Nevertheless we are glad to see, especially in recent years, that more and more people are rejecting outdated ideas and attempting instead to come to their own conclusions about both the origins of the ancient civilizations and the discovery of the New World; and all we can do here is to offer you the benefit of our own conclusions and discoveries so that you can decide what the most probable answer is to a particular problem. At the same time this is our own contribution to investigations into man's fascinating past!

# PART ONE

# Prehistory

# Chapter One

A journey through history—artificial mutations?—hominids and apes?—did giants exist?—sensational discoveries?

Perhaps the best way of describing this book might be to call it "a journey through the history of the earth and its inhabitants". By studying prehistory, evolution, mutations, ancient civilizations, megaliths, Atlantis and numerous other subjects we believe we have found satisfactory answers to a number of questions which have given rise to thousands of different theories throughout the centuries.

We are all given to wondering about our early ancestors and how the human race came into existence, yet in spite of our achievements we have very little idea of what human evolution really involved. Some writers explain or deny man's evolution by means of myths and legends which cannot be verified, while others believe that it was brought about by visits from extraterrestrial "cosmonauts". The mythological stories are discussed later on in this book; but what can we say about the cosmonauts at this stage?

We agree with a good deal of what other writers have had to say on the subject, in that they all assume that something must have existed before the first civilizations known to us which brought them into being. These writers spend a good deal of time trying to link cosmonauts with these early civilizations; yet other possibilities must be borne in mind.

Without wanting to seem too sceptical or too prejudiced towards other people's theories we do nonetheless find it hard to accept the following ideas which are advanced by these writers: that cosmonauts may have caused human evolution; that they might have artificially fertilized female beings; that they chose terrestrial organisms for artificial mutations, and that by mutation they deliberately turned hominids into men; that female beings were artificially produced; that they undertook the breeding of living beings in distillation plant or test tubes; and that primitive man preceded woman.

*    *    *

Everything must have a beginning, so what could be more sensible than to begin our investigations in prehistory? This period is also very important to those writers who favour cosmic theories since they too make it their starting-point, but while these writers are very skilled in the art of persuasion we hope to convince by reason combined with a scientific approach. We feel that if we were to depart entirely from scientific method and rely on old traditions alone we would instantly lose our grip on reality. It may be that these traditions were originally based on actual events, and that they have been transformed down the centuries as a result of being transmitted orally from generation to generation.

Perhaps you are familiar with the game in which one person sitting in a circle with other people starts to tell a story to his neighbour who then recounts it to *his* neighbour and so on; and when the story has gone the full circle it comes out in a quite different version from the original. One person may add to the story, while another will leave out parts, not only because memory is fallible but also because we are so used to giving our own versions of a story when we cannot remember it accurately. For this reason we cannot use oral traditions as a point of departure, though we should certainly take them into account!

The development of all living creatures, from the simplest to the most complex, is known to science as evolution, Charles Darwin was the pioneer in this field: his achievements are enormous, although we can see in retrospect that the theory of the origin of species was not entirely his own discovery.

Changes in the world's flora and fauna are due to what science nowadays terms mutations, most of which are either harmful or useless and disappear after a short time, though they may bring about sudden alterations in a species. However, in the struggle

18

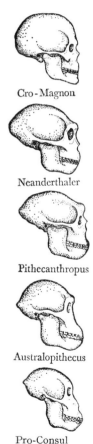

Cro-Magnon

Neanderthaler

Pithecanthropus

Australopithecus

Pro-Consul

Fig. 1.
The Evolution of Man.

These sketches show you only the most important groups and it represents the simplest version of the family tree, beginning with Pro-Consul ape at the bottom of the series of fossil skulls. There are variants within these clearly distinct classes and some skulls found have proved difficult to place in any of the categories. Not all discoveries can be clearly dated, so that the construction of the family tree is complicated if one attempts to take into account all the variants. For these reasons many books on this subject show differing classifications.

for survival these mutations can have considerable effect if they coincide with or correspond to modifications in the climate, living conditions and so forth; and if they are inherited by the next generation they will gradually form a new attribute in a species. Thanks to this automatic and at the same time creative power of adaptation—which was Darwin's real discovery—the shapes and forms of all species are as we find them today.

However, it is not possible to follow the course of evolution by studying mutations alone. For example, in order to gain some insight into human evolution it is necessary to classify as accurately as possible all the available evidence of fossil men and any remains of creatures resembling human beings, and to arrange these in chronological order. According to some "experts" one can say nothing with any degree of certainty about fossil remains because if one does, the dating and placing of already established material immediately becomes suspect. But this really is putting the cart before the horse: it is true that, as a result of fresh evidence, a limited number of finds sometimes have to be re-ordered on the ladder of human evolution, and that occasionally well-established dates and locations have to be revised, but the most important question is that of *relative age*, and here radical alterations are infrequent. It is regrettable that people still think it necessary to refer to "missing links" and that in spite of the ever-increasing amount of material available they keep to their pet theories.

We must take it for granted that our planet is a part of the universe, and that it must have originated in the universe; and so it might easily be supposed that man, too, has his origins in the universe—but such a conclusion could well be premature. Even if there were beings somewhere in space with similar ways of thinking and perceiving to ourselves, it does not necessarily follow that they would have any physical resemblance to us, since the environment to which they were accustomed would in all likelihood be quite different from the earth. It seems reasonable that we should confine ourselves to the study of human evolution on the assumption that man is a product of terrestrial development, and not just a link in a chain that has its origins elsewhere in space.

The belief that human evolution from the animal kingdom may *never* be proved is still fairly widely held; yet proof that he did so is only too clear and convincing—and it is by no means based entirely on fossils!

If people believe that man has always existed in his present form, then it seems logical to ask where we might find the fossil remains of these people; yet no such remains exist! Nevertheless remains *have* certainly been found indicating a pattern of evolution from a common ancestor which leads on the one hand to mankind and on the other to various species of ape—developments that seem only too obvious!

The fact that many people do not take these proofs seriously is not something for which science is to blame. It often happens that those with least knowledge of the subject oppose the theory of evolution most strongly—frequently because of religious convictions—while others are willing enough to acknowledge that evolution applies to animals, but not to human beings. They want to exempt man entirely from its workings, and this we consider somewhat illogical.

Again, people often say that science impedes its own progress by rejecting every contrary opinion in its determination to uphold the theory of evolution at all costs. Most people don't believe this nonsense, realizing that it is not a question of science being complacent and inflexible or clinging stubbornly to outmoded ideas: concrete evidence is to be preferred to vague abstractions, especially those which are becoming fashionable today, though this should not prevent us from speculating about new evidence. Science means *searching* for the truth, complete with faults, wrong solutions and misguided lines of investigation!

However receptive one may be to new ideas one only too often comes up against those which are based solely on wild fantasies, legends and faulty interpretations of facts, often accompanied by all kinds of misleading inaccuracies; and this occurs a great deal where the classification and naming of fossil remains are concerned. Too frequently one gets the impression that the various discoveries are all so very different from each other that it is impossible to get a clear and accurate overall picture of them; if one also remembers that the important finds are frequently obscured by less important issues and pieces of evidence, and that the chronology is often confused or concealed, it is no wonder that the ill-informed student of the subject tends to get lost and to accept dubious and alien ideas.

For these reasons it is worth discussing the evidence for evolution in some detail, though the subject is so vast that we shall only mention those discoveries which shed the most light on the story; yet in doing so we shall not entirely ignore those writers who believe that mankind originated elsewhere in space.

Man is not descended from any form of ape living today. All organisms living at the present day are the end products of their particular lines of development; the descent of related species can be traced back to a common ancestor of an earlier period, so that although the apes we see today in zoos or in the wild can in no way be considered our ancestors, we do of course have distant cousins in the so-called "anthropoidal" apes such as the gibbon, orang-outang, gorilla and chimpanzee, all of which have no tail and ultimately share a common ancestry with man.

If we go far enough back in time, say thirty or forty million years ago to the Oligocene period, we find that even the anthropoid ape was not yet in existence. The remains of various sorts of small ape have been found dating from that time in the El Fayum valley in Egypt, a rich source of fossilized mammalian bones. These small creatures resemble their predecessors, the so-called "half-apes", which themselves remind one in many respects of squirrels, though their teeth were very similar to those of the human being (see fig. 2). It is not absolutely clear which tooth should be thought of as the canine, a subject on which opinions still vary.

It would of course be nonsense to suggest that this small ape was some kind of early man, though this idea has been put forward; the creature was an ape and nothing else.

But other more anthropoidal apes from later deposits in this valley justify the claim that here we have the ancestors of the gibbon, the first of the anthropoidal apes with human characteristics to branch off from the other apes. In tracing the evolu-

22

tion of man, the most important problem has been to find the ape which must have been the ancestor of the anthropoids as well as the forerunner of *Homo sapiens*.

Apes possessing these characteristics have been discovered in many parts of the Old World, such as, for example, the various species of *Dryopithecus*, which are roughly twenty-five million years old. The important thing to note in this respect is the Y5 pattern of the molar teeth, which is common only to men and anthropoids.

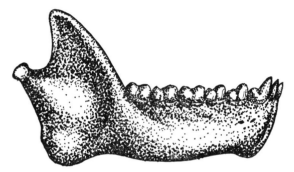

Fig. 2. The lower jaw of the primitive ape Parapithecus from the El Fayum-valley.

These tailless apes lived on the ground and no longer in the trees, and already walked upright to some extent. Various branches of these anthropoids are known, leading not only to man and present-day anthropoids but also to several species which are now extinct.

The origin of another very large extinct anthropoid which came from southern China is still not clear, but it appears to have had nothing to do with human ancestry; yet people often discuss this ape as if its remains were those of an early human giant, and that they were acknowledged as such by scientists. What is the truth about this creature? It is worth discussing this discovery in some detail since the considerable misunderstanding it has aroused has been to some extent brought about by science itself.

When the Dutch palaeontologist Professor von Koenigswald

23

went in search of fossil teeth—the so-called "dragon's teeth", which were sold as highly efficacious medicines in many Chinese drug-stores—he discovered several molars like those of human beings but of an unknown size in Hong Kong and Canton. These teeth were far larger than human or apes' teeth, whether fossil or present-day; the molars are as much as one third larger than those of the Java "giant", twice the size of those of Java man and—taking the crowns and roots of the teeth together—a

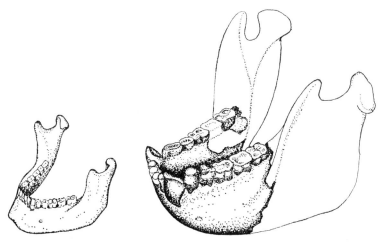

Fig. 3.   A reconstruction of the lower jaw of Gigantopithecus. (right) the largest of all apes' jaws, compared with (left) the lower jaw of a modern man.

good five or six times the size of the teeth of a present-day human being. They display no great similarities to the teeth of fossil or recent anthropoids but they do bear a closer resemblance to those of modern man (fig. 3) than do the teeth of the fossil Java and Peking man.

Von Koenigswald assumed that the teeth belonged to an as yet undiscovered ape of huge size which he accordingly called *Gigantopithecus*, meaning giant ape. Weidenreich and other experts who studied Von Koenigswald's work stressed the human aspects of the find, but the material available at this stage was insufficient to allow any further conclusions to be drawn. However, matters changed in 1955 when Weng Chung Pei discovered forty-seven teeth belonging to the same creature in the southern Chinese provinces of Kwangtung and Kwangsi; and during an expedition organized by the Sinica Academy from 1956 to 1958, an enormous number of fossils was found in a cave in Kwangsi, among them three more or less complete lower jaws. At the same time more than a thousand molars were assembled from various sources, as a result of which the overall picture became much clearer.

*Gigantopithecus* appears to have been a very large anthropoid with moderate size canines; it certainly lived on the ground but probably did not walk erect. His actual height has not yet been determined.

There is no definite relationship between the size of an animal and the size of its teeth and lower jaw, so it is not possible to say how large *Gigantopithecus* was on the basis of its molars and lower jaw alone. It must in any case have been bigger than a gorilla, and it may have resembled a larger and heavier orangoutang. Its size is still a matter of debate; some people reckon that it must have been around 2·70 metres in height, which may not be far from the truth.

For a long time the age of the southern Chinese *Gigantopithecus* was not known but it is now assumed that it lived between 500,000 and 1,000,000 years ago. *Gigantopithecus* is clearly unrelated to *Homo sapiens*; but none of its bones have been found apart from the molars and lower jaw.

Some years ago in India, a precursor of *Gigantopithecus* was discovered which appeared to be several million years old since the deposits in which its jaw had been found were between five and nine million years of age.

It has been established, then, that the Chinese "giant" was in fact a large ape; it would certainly be incorrect to say that it has been accepted by scientists as a human giant.

One of the other "giants" put on show from time to time is the Java "giant", which refers to the jawbone remains of *Meganthropus*—meaning a man of gigantic proportions (fig. 4)—but the full implications of this discovery are as yet far from clear. Remains

25

have been found in very ancient deposits in Java, some of them by Von Koenigswald.

Despite the strength of the jawbone, these remains clearly belong to a group of creatures which were closer to human beings than to the various species of ape. Von Koenigswald and many others consider *Meganthropus* to be a forerunner of Java and Peking men, both of which were "true" humans. Several writers

Fig. 4. A lower jaw fragment of Meganthropus (2) the "Giant of Java". Despite the small but solid fragment it cannot be claimed that whatever was attached to it constituted a "giant"!

have assumed a height of 2·50 metres for *Meganthropus*, but until an upper or lower bone has been found this must remain a matter of speculation, as in the case of *Gigantopithecus*!

In 1964 three samples of *Meganthropus* remains were compared with similar material from the Olduvai Gorge in East Africa. According to the experts both sets of specimens show the same grade of hominigation, and these creatures probably lived at the same time, between one and two million years ago. In any case *Meganthropus* was a human-like creature or a primitive kind of man. A comparison of its jawbone remains with ones from South Africa—and we possess dozens of such jaws and skulls—shows that the cranial capacity of the Java "giant" cannot have been specially large: the cubic capacity of the South African anthropoid skulls (scientifically known as *Australopithecines*) is only of the order of 500 to 600 cubic centimetres, whereas a modern man's brain size is on average about 1450.

It is clear then that we are not talking about creatures intelligent enough to have great technical skill and knowledge, as is so often claimed; but these creatures were certainly capable of making stone tools of a very primitive sort.

To sum up about the Java "giant": *Meganthropus* has unmistakable resemblances to *Australopithecus*, and its skull capacity hardly exceeded that of the great apes. As we have seen, the actual size of *Meganthropus* is still unknown, but the related *Australopithecines* are now thought to have been little more than 1·20 to 1·50 metres high.

Yet another "giant" which is often discussed is the South

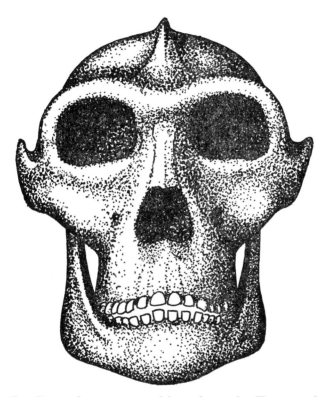

Fig. 5. Paranthropus crassidens from the Transvaal, an hominid with the gorilla-type skull ridge.

African (Transvaal) specimen, two of which (*Paranthropus robustus* and *Paranthropus crassidens*: see fig. 5) are often confused. *Paranthropus* (i.e. near man) must have been a vegetarian, judging from the completely worn-down state of its teeth. In the specimens found at Swartkrans the muscles employed in chewing were so highly developed that there was an extra long crest on the

27

roof of the skull to which these were attached—a feature it shares with the gorilla. The brain area is quite small in relation to the face as a whole, but unfortunately there is no skull of this species complete enough to give us an accurate estimate of brain size: bearing in mind the cranial crest and the large jaws it would seem that its brain capacity differed little from that of the gorilla, and judging by the fragmentary remains of bone, its likely height was around 1·50 metres. The females were smaller and slimmer.

*Paranthropus* appears to have remained unchanged for a million years or so; according to Robinson, one of the most important workers in this field, this may have been the result of his never using stone tools.

The South African "giant", *Paranthropus*, now classed as *Australopithecus robustus*, belongs in spite of his human attributes to an off-shoot of our line of evolution which has since died out.

It is interesting to examine the reasons why people have believed in the existence of giants throughout the centuries; indeed, many people still believe in them, if the various books published recently on the subject are anything to go by. Were it not for this willingness to believe one would never hear fossil finds described as evidence for the existence of giants at some stage in our past; nor would it have been suggested that at some stage in his past man was visited by "gigantic cosmonauts" and "unique individuals".

Many stories were told in previous centuries of people who had seen giants on their travels through distant and foreign lands, and many writers today look to these tales for evidence that giants actually existed. What is peculiar about all this is that the height attributed to these creatures usually varied from 2·10 to 2·70 metres, and that in nearly every case these "giants" were seen by travellers on their first voyages of discovery and never again after that. Quite apart from the trustworthiness of such observations, it is worth remembering that skeletal remains of "giant men" have never been found anywhere; and that those remains which have been used to prove the existence of giants have been wrongly interpreted, often deliberately so. Some of these misinterpretations have already been discussed, but it may be advisable to say a little more on the subject.

We can begin by introducing an author* who deals with the discovery in Spring Valley in Eureka, Nevada, of a "giant's bone", which people remembered as having been found in July 1887 by four men searching for gold. Although physicians from Eureka believed it to be a human bone, this is no reason for assuming it to be that of a giant; and on closer inspection, the whole matter looks like amusing nonsense.

The bone was supposed to have been broken off *above* the knee, and it measured exactly ninety-nine centimetres from the knee to the heel; if this really was the case then it most probably was a thigh-bone, but it could also have been a shin or calf-bone! We must assume then that it was broken off *below* the knee, but since it is difficult to imagine that the length could be determined solely from the upper part (the knee-joint), we have to conclude that only the shin-bone or calf-bone had been found with the upper part missing.

But then we must ask how it could possibly be maintained that the bone measured exactly ninety-nine centimetres from the knee to the heel (the lowest part of the heel-bone), since it is impossible to assess the total length with any accuracy if parts are missing. Without wanting to attack the author it does seem that this is an excellent example of the kind of reasoning we have described: the whole approach is confused, and as a result the reader is left with nothing more than the "fact" of the discovery of a "giant's bone", while the improbability of it is not discussed.

But there are two sides to every question. Fossilized footprints were reported from Brayton, Tennessee; they were alleged to be those of a human being with six toes and feet about thirty-three centimetres long. It would be possible to indulge in any amount of wild speculations about such a find but there is a reasonable explanation in the fact that when one walks on soft soil or sand one's footprints often expand to a greater length than usual, and if this is accompanied by some lateral movement

* *They came from Other Planets*, P. Kolosimo, p. 130.

29

as well, the imprint left may give the impression that one has more than one's normal number of toes!

Another story concerns a sarcophagus which was said to have been found at Crittenden in Arizona in 1891 and to have contained a human being of sorts three metres long and with six toes on each foot; similarly it was reported that Russian anthropologists in the Caucasus had found skeletons of between 2·80 and 3·12 metres long. One's reaction to both stories is the same: one merely wants to know where these specimens are now. One can hardly presume that scientists have gone to work in such an irresponsible manner that their discoveries have been destroyed, yet nobody can show us any material evidence, or even photographs or drawings!

The same objections apply to the two "enormous molars" which were supposed to have been found in a coalmine known as Eagle No. 3 at Bear Creek in Montana in 1920. These teeth were, it was claimed, three times the size of normal human teeth, and had been discovered in deposits at least thirty million years old. And there have been reports of other mines containing similar human remains of comparable antiquity—reports which have been followed immediately by protestations that science systematically denies the validity of such claims. Yet it is right that scientists should remain sceptical, since the whereabouts of the evidence is unknown: we are prepared to acknowledge the importance of such finds and would even admit the existence of giants, but not on hearsay alone!

Perhaps one should consider all these reports from America against the background of the "theory", already long-established, that the earliest types of human being came from that continent; but although America has been termed a land of limitless possibilities there is not a single proof to support this theory, nor even any controversial discovery.

Prehistoric tools have been found nearly all over the world, among them large numbers of heavy hand-axes which, because of their massive measurements, have immediately been connected with "giants". For example, hand-axes weighing around eight kilos have been unearthed among flint tools and other remains in Agadir: and it is at once assumed that these implements could only have been handled by creatures about four metres high!

In the first place, it is important to remember that when archaeologists talk about sites where implements were manufactured they are not thinking in terms of large enterprises, involving buildings and huge quantities of tools. A site is more likely to be a fairly small area in which flakes, unfinished stone tools and their new raw materials have been discovered. There would be little difficulty in finding pieces of half-finished stone which had been thrown carelessly away because they had fractured or because the implement maker had realized that the material was not of the best quality; yet these stones—and even larger ones from which pieces had been broken—give some people the erroneous idea that these "hand-axes" (as they imagine them to be!) could only be managed by "giants" with enormous hands. Of course large hand-axes existed in prehistoric times, but the fact that these tools might have been wielded in *both* hands appears to have escaped those who champion the existence of giants. In our own era we have used wood axes which needed to be held with both hands!

The term "hand-axe" originated in the early days of archaeological investigations into fossil remains, but when it was learned later that much bigger tools had been used the word was rightly replaced by "biface" to describe tools worked equally on both sides. The fact that the word "hand-axe" is current in a popular sense does not mean that all these tools were held in one hand only!

Finally we must remember that medical science is able to provide explanations for several peculiarities in growth which may make people into "giants". Now and again we come across cases of enormous growth which are really tragic examples of abnormality due to deviations in the structure of certain hormones. These are known to doctors and others as *acromegaly* and gigantism: for example, the so-called "giant" of Alton, Illinois, reached a height of 2·70 metres, and there was the Irish giant O'Brien who was seven feet tall.

Some people like to believe that by mating abnormally large human beings one could breed a race of giants. Experiments in this area have been carried out in animals, some of which reached twice their normal size after injections; the only difficulty was that they never reached maturity and so were unable to breed!

# Chapter Two

The Piltdown hoax—anthropoids and hominids—the club
as a weapon; stone tools—when was fire first used?—
Neanderthal man; the first to bury his dead—apes with a
cranial capacity of 1100 cubic centimetres?

Having dealt with so-called "giants", "ape-like men" and other
reputedly "sensational discoveries", we can now examine human
prehistory; and we will begin with the Piltdown skull, not because it played a true part in the story of evolution—it was a very
clever hoax—but because the rejection of this discovery had so
long-lasting an influence to too great an extent upon many people.

The story of the Piltdown hoax was and still is sometimes used
to undermine belief in other fossil finds. The possibility of other
discoveries being suspect seemed greater once the Piltdown skull
had been proved to be a forgery, and some people felt that they
were justified in throwing overboard any theory which relied on
fossil remains. Thus one often hears it said that the whole business of *Eoanthropus* (the Piltdown skull) should serve as a pretext for re-examining what we mean by the truth and by reliable
evidence.

The story as it is usually told contains many inaccuracies and
for that reason it is worth making one or two observations about
the whole affair.

It is not true to say that our account of man's descent was
seriously misled by this so-called "important find". We examined
numerous books and scientific articles dealing with the Piltdown
skull as well as works written before the forgery was exposed,
and we have compared the various scholars' conclusions with
each other. It become clear that at the time the experts were
reluctant to believe that the skull provided useful evidence of
the pattern of evolution, and it was in fact rejected as dubious

evidence. To speak of a deception that lasted for forty years is to put things too strongly.

Furthermore it would be a mistake to believe that the first part of the skull to be found was that of a carefully prepared orang-outang skull; in fact, the first things to be discovered were the fossilized skull bones of a modern man, their only peculiarity being that they were fairly thick—which can be explained by the disorder known as Paget's Disease. The lower jaw fragment turned out to be that of an orang-outang, as many eminent scholars had already suspected, and the bogus canine tooth looked exactly as one might imagine it would under the circumstances. After the discovery of the lower jaw minus the canine some scholars were able to deduce what the canine would have looked like, so it is not difficult to imagine their amazement when shortly afterwards a canine answering in every way to their reconstruction was actually found. Several experts took this as proof that the skull was genuine, but most authorities completely rejected the find. This skull and several fragments from another were studied and written about with meticulous care by Sir Arthur Keith, who virtually made it his life's work because of his conviction that all the parts belonged together.

In the light of subsequent fossil finds it became increasingly difficult to believe that this strange combination of a modern-looking skull and an anthropoid lower jaw could be genuine, so some years after the find the British Museum undertook an extensive investigation which clearly demonstrated that the Piltdown skull was a hoax. It is often said that the man who found the bones—the solicitor and amateur archaeologist Dawson—was the guilty party, but in fact no inquiry as to who was really to blame was ever carried out, Dawson having already been dead for many years by this time; and it is quite possible that far from being its perpetrator, he was himself a victim of the hoax.

* &ast; &ast;

Having looked at the Piltdown affair, we must now turn our attention to the hominids, who were our real ancestors.

In the world of science these human-like creatures are known as Australopithecines, a name that had been given to the fossilized skull of a child at a time when it was not certain whether the skull in question was that of a chimpanzee-like ape or a creature with the characterisitics of an ape. Its discoverer, Dart, assumed the skull to be that of a human being and cautiously gave it the name *Australopithecus africanus*, which simply means "Southern Ape of Africa" (see plates 1 and 2). At first the scientific world reacted very coolly indeed to this important discovery; but it was soon to cause a great deal of interest through the fact that its teeth, which had been studied in detail, were very much like those of a human being.

But the matter was finally settled some years later when a number of adult *Australopithecus* skulls and jaw fragments was found. These skulls have a very small cranial capacity, hardly any greater than that of the anthropoids, but whereas the large and heavy jaw resembles that of an ape, the teeth themselves, which lack the prominent canines normally associated with the apes, betray the fact that what we have here really is a human type of creature.

The later discovery of other skeletal remains demonstrated that these creatures could already walk completely erect. The best known reconstructed skeleton is that of a young and slightly built woman who was only 1·20 metres tall.

The adult *Australopithecus* was at first given the name of *Plesianthropus* (plate 3) since it was thought that it differed in important respects from the *Australopithecus* child found previously, but today this term is hardly used any more. These men-like creatures are thought to have lived about two million years ago.

Similar beings have also been found in the Olduvai Gorge in East Africa. These are somewhat more human and because of this they have been called, perhaps a little prematurely, *Homo habilis* by the man who found them, Dr L. S. B. Leakey. In shape they are completely human, but their brains only really began to develop when *Homo sapiens* began to break away from the animal kingdom. Too much importance should not be attached to the discovery of *Homo habilis* (the specific name "habilis" is taken from the Latin, meaning "able, handy, mentally skilful, vigorous"), since many inexpert visionaries and even some well-meaning writers tend to exaggerate its importance because Leakey thought that this kind of *Australopithecus* belongs to a new species of the genus *Homo*.

Despite his tendency to seek publicity Leaky was a leading

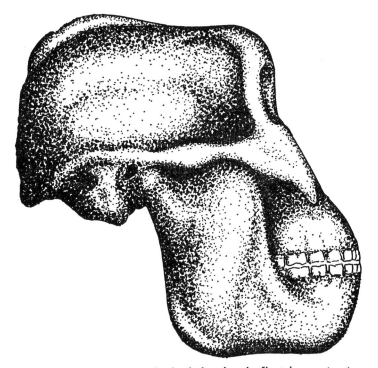

Fig. 6.   Zinjanthropus boisei, Leakey's first important find, and also appropriately known as "Nutcracker Man".

researcher in this field, who contributed to an exceptional degree to our knowledge of the past; yet he was obliged on purely scientific grounds to modify many of his claims. It is not true to say that Leakey dealt a mortal blow to the old theories, since despite his ideas about *Zinjanthropus* (fig. 6; plate 4) and *Homo habilis*—which have been known for quite some time now—he has clearly lost some ground in the struggle for scientific recognition; but nevertheless it remains beyond dispute that Leakey has considerably enriched science with his invaluable specimens of apes and hominids.

*Homo habilis*, then, was a rather more advanced type of *Australopithecus*; he was already capable of tool-making, though care must be exercised in the use of this word. It is not true, for instance—though it is commonly believed to be the case—that they made axes and hoes out of stone and pieces of rock; for a long time it was not even certain that the first anthropoids made stone implements at all, though this has in fact been shown to be the case in a number of sites. The stones used were generally

Fig. 7.  An Australopithecus stone tool from Olduvai Gorge, East Africa.

pebbles which were easy enough to hold in the hand and from which a more or less sharp edge could be obtained by striking pieces off (fig. 7). It could be said that such an object need not be a tool at all, since it may have been fashioned that way by natural causes; and no doubt, these men used ready-made splinters and other sharp fragments, and the search for such splinters would have preceded the discovery that they could be manufactured. Yet the modified stones found were real tools, for they had a certain uniformity about them and they were discovered on dwelling-sites among remnants of broken animal-bones; and they were often made of a carefully selected hard type of stone which did not come from the immediate surroundings.

Incidentally it should also be remarked that it is not true that tools made of stone—or indeed of other materials—first came into use around forty thousand years ago. Even chimpanzees in the wild make use of clubs and other weapons to defend

37

themselves against leopards, while the *Australopithecines* used the bones, jaws and horns of antelopes killed by themselves or by hyenas. Similarly many baboon skulls have been unearthed, cracked or shattered by a hard blow from a club. The *Australopithecines* probably lived and hunted in groups since otherwise they could not have preyed upon solidly organized groups of baboons.

Again there is often some confusion about the terms anthropoid and hominid: the former denotes such apes as the gorilla, chimpanzee, orang-outang, together with now extinct species such as Pro-Consul and *Dryopithecus*, whereas hominids are man-like creatures, including the extinct *Paranthropus* and the *Australopithecines*—though it should be emphasized that the first of these certainly did not give rise to the line that leads to modern man.

As we have seen, *Australopithecus* lived in Africa, but he could have occurred elsewhere in the world; yet it is important to emphasize that only *one* species finally led to *Homo sapiens*. It is worth stressing this because people often say that man's immediate ancestors were to be found in various parts of the globe and that this accounts for different races found in the world today. In fact present-day races are a comparatively recent development: our present racial traits only become apparent at the end of the last Ice Age.

Arguing from this misconception, people have talked about the "intellectual superiority" of the white races—a pernicious doctrine, all the more so since the idea of the Aryan "*Herrenvolk*" is still so fresh in the memory.

Many publicity-seeking popular writers state that the cranial capacity of our ancestors was not more than 600 to 700 cubic centimetres; while some go further and maintain that because the gorilla has much the same brain capacity as our ancestors did, they must have had a similar intelligence and potential to the gorilla.

People try to lessen the significance of man's ancestors—such as the *Australopithecines*—with statements of this kind; yet they may not be so far wrong as far as intelligence is concerned. Intellectual ability does not only depend on the brain capacity of the skull, so a comparison with the gorilla is somewhat far-fetched since it is very difficult for us to assess the potential of these animals when they live in the wild; we cannot take those living apathetic and unnatural lives in zoos as criteria. The abilities of the *Australopithecines* were definitely higher than a gorilla's, since their erect posture left them with their hands free to make and use all sorts of tools. Napier has demonstrated that the hands of *Homo habilis* differed little from those of the young gorilla; they were unable to use their hands as well as we modern men can. Put very briefly, the only differences between *Australopithecus* and an anthropoid are his two-footed, erect gait and his dentition, which was very striking in that it was fundamentally already very like our own.

In addition to the terms hominid and anthropoid one often picks up references to "ape man" or "primitive man", terms which are used without any clear explanation and which need to be defined more precisely.

*Homo erectus* (i.e. walking erect) forms the next stage in man's family tree after *Australopithecus*.

Representative remains were first found in Java in 1891 by Dubois, a Dutch doctor, who dubbed them *Pithecanthropus erectus*. The name was chosen by Dubois because the skull was flat and anthropoidal (plate 5) and its cranial capacity was fairly small—around 990 cubic centimetres. Along with the roof of the skull he found a perfectly formed human thigh-bone.

If the two belonged together, and there is no reason to doubt that they did, it proved that this creature—which lived about two million years ago—was already walking perfectly upright, con-trary to beliefs current at the time when it was found. More complete skulls and jaws were found later in Java: *Pithecanthropus* became known as Java man, and was estimated to be around 700,000 years old (plate 6).

The discovery in 1927 of *Sinanthropus pekinensis* (Peking man) was very important. He lived about 400,000 years ago and was already using fire, as we see from the layers of ash several feet thick found in the caves in which he lived: it is not true to say

39

that human beings only began to make use of fire about 40,000 years ago, as is often claimed. Twelve skulls and other remains of about forty examples of Peking man were found, but they disappeared during the Second World War. Fortunately there are numerous casts and photographs of this primitive type of man (plate 7).

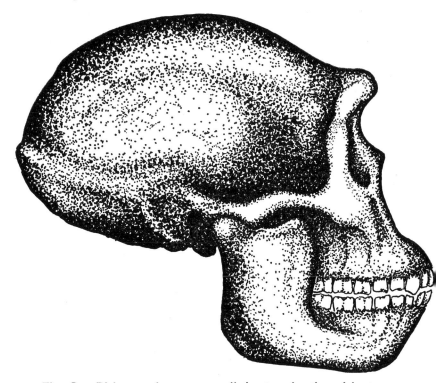

Fig. 8. Pithecanthropus modjokertensis, the oldest representative of the Homo erectus group.

It was on the basis of this material that one of the excavators, the Jesuit priest, Teilhard de Chardin, attempted to explain man in his profound philosophical theories, and to bridge the gap between evolution and the Church.

As we have seen, both *Pithecanthropus* and *Sinanthropus* belong to the *Homo erectus* group (fig. 8), as do other finds such as the so-called "Chellean man", *Africanthropus* and the trio of *Atlanthropus* lower jaws from North Africa. The Heidelberg lower jaw and an occipital bone from Hungary also belong to this group.

The cranial capacity of these men ranged from about 800 to 1200 cubic centimetres, and their stone implements have been found throughout almost the whole world. These tools are less crude than those of their more primitive forerunners.

After *Pithecanthropus* comes the much better-known Neanderthal man. It is often claimed that the discoverer of Neanderthal man, Fuhlrott, assembled a complete skeleton from incomplete remains; however this does not agree with the facts, since not all the necessary anatomical evidence was available at that time. The name itself, *Homo neanderthalensis*, was suggested in 1864, but was not in general use until the turn of the century.

It is incorrect to associate Fuhlrott with the dating of Neanderthal man, who existed between 80,000 and 120,000 years ago. Fuhlrott himself had no idea how old the bones that he had found were, but he was bold enough to suggest that they pre-dated the Flood.

Fuhlrott was a modest man and had little to do with the Ape-man theory, which was the work of the few scholars of the period who were convinced of the importance of the find.

Strangely enough the first specimens of adult Neanderthal men were not found on the actual Neanderthal site itself, since an almost complete skull (see fig. 9) of this type was discovered in a cave at Gibraltar during the construction of some fortification works in 1848. At the time it was generally believed that the skull was that of a woman from the very distant past, and since the matter was dropped the discovery never acquired the scientific attention it deserved. The Gibraltar Scientific Society made a note of it in its proceedings of March 3rd 1848, but after that it was totally forgotten. Even the circumstances surrounding its discovery were forgotten, and it is a marvellous piece of luck that the skull still exists today.

One of the most important characteristics of this Neanderthal skull is the pronounced ridge over the eyes, which is absent in

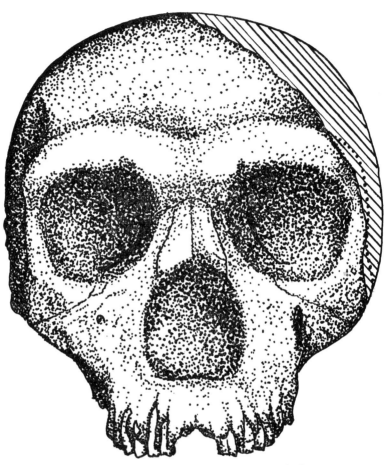

Fig. 9. This Gibraltar skull was the first adult
Neanderthal discovered.

modern man. The round eye-sockets are very large and the nose
very broad. The teeth are extremely worn but appear to have
been massive in build and of considerable length.

It is interesting that the middle incisors are missing. According to experts these teeth were forcibly removed long before their
owner died, reminiscent of the ceremonial custom of certain
Negro tribes, Australian aborigines and other primitive peoples
by which incisors are compulsorily extracted even today.

Neanderthal man lived in the period preceding and up to the middle of the last Ice Age, i.e. 30,000 to 110,000 years ago.

"Fossil man", the famous French palaeontologist Cuvier said at the beginning of the last century, "does not exist". He said this because he had been shown numerous relics of ape-like human remains consisting without exception of peculiarities and rarities; and during the first half of the nineteenth century those who were unwilling to acknowledge the existence of primitive races other than those alive today quoted his words wherever they felt it to be necessary, even though this was not what he meant at all. Today the remains of over one hundred Neanderthalers—as well as those of yet older beings—have been unearthed, and nobody any longer thinks these relics worthy of controversy. We know that these primitive beings similar to men did exist, and the approximate dates of all the important stages in man's descent have been decided on, yet as we have seen evolutionary doctrine is still found by some extremely difficult to accept.

To return to the Neanderthalers: they were very robust, of average size and not as different from present-day human beings as used to be thought, although their bones were sometimes rather thick and crooked. The skull, too, had some rather primitive qualities such as the pronounced anthropoidal eyebrow ridge already mentioned, a flat forehead and a receding chin (plate 8).

Neanderthal man was the first to practise burial of the dead; his burials clearly show that a great deal of care went into this, the departed being supplied with gifts and ornaments. Burial resulted from a feeling of piety towards the deceased; at the same time the body could not become a prey to wild animals. Belief in a hereafter therefore seems probable and there is certainly evidence of a sense of such values as love, faith, friendship and awe; yet this is surprising when one remembers that the Neanderthalers practised cannibalism, as we know from the fact that skulls were often opened by force for the purpose of brain extraction.

The stone tools used by Neanderthal man have been found in

thousands—tens of thousands, in fact. They are very varied, being manufactured with a special new technique, and it is thought that many of them were used for scraping the hides of animals, to judge from their razor-like qualities. This would suggest clothing, which would be absolutely essential in view of the severe climatic conditions in Europe.

It should be pointed out that the Neanderthalers did not appear solely in Europe; they, or men very like them, were to be found everywhere except America. However they created none of the famous cave drawings as is sometimes claimed: these were the work of *Homo sapiens* (modern man) and not of the Neanderthalers.

It will be clear by now that with all these fossil finds to go on—and we have mentioned only a few of them—it would be misleading to claim that fossilized human remains are so few and far between that all reconstructions of what our ancestors were like are based on nothing more than a "poor heap of bones". We would like to emphasize that this whole science is built on solid fact rather than on controversial hypotheses.

Apart from Cro-Magnon man and the Neanderthalers, no complete skeletons of other prehistoric men have been found. With regard to "incomplete" skeletons it should be noted that whenever a specimen is found with only one arm or leg we can obviously deduce how the other must have looked. Although some people oppose the doctrines of evolution, all the evidence goes to show that man has clearly developed from a species of ape. Occasionally one comes across writers who proudly assert that apes with a cranial capacity of 1100 to 1200 cubic centimetres or more have never been discovered, and they take this as proof that man has nothing in common with apes of any kind since his brain size is so superior. Apes with a brain capacity of this kind have never existed, since they hardly ever go as high as 650 cubic centimetres; any anthropoidal skulls with a brain capacity bigger than this can be regarded at once as being of a primitive human sort.

Having mentioned the skull sizes of the apes, some of these writers go on to show that the human cranial capacity is, as we know, far greater—around 1500 to 1600 cubic centimetres. But this is to exaggerate; the average size of the skull of a modern man is about 1450 cubic centimetres, with the limits as far as normal people are concerned running from around 900 to 2250! As far as intelligence goes there may be no great differences within these limits.

We are treating prehistoric man at some length in this and the following chapter in order to put our ideas about him into correct perspective in view of all the publications in which entirely erroneous notions have been aired and terminologies confused. But above all we have attempted to show that the development of man has been a very gradual process, beginning with Pro-Consul 25,000,000 years ago and the Australopithecines about 2,000,000 years ago. Everything points to the fact that our evolution has lasted millions of years, and that a period of ten thousand years is not long in comparison. Bearing this in mind, together with the slow processes of physical and mental evolution, we find that during the last few thousand years of our history some sensational and spectacular phenomena have occurred. What can explain the extremely rapid change from a prehistoric state to a level of civilization such as those reached by the ancient cultures around the Mediterranean?

# Chapter Three

When did modern man arise?—where did Cro-Magnon man come from, and where did he go to?—were the cave paintings done by "barbarians"?—why were they painted?

*Homo sapiens* certainly succeeded the Neanderthal man, but he cannot have descended directly from him; this conclusion is almost unavoidable if one examines the Neanderthalers in some detail, since they managed to survive in Western Europe until 30,000 years ago and their cave remains lie immediately beneath those of *Homo sapiens*.

In the long run, though, the Neanderthalers seem to have led nowhere as far as the development of man is concerned; in this context it is interesting to note that the Neanderthalers from Eastern Europe and the Near East appear to have been more like *Homo sapiens*. A mixing of the races seems to have taken place among those discovered in Palestine by Miss Garrod, but it is important to realize that Neanderthal man forms a variety of the family tree of man and is not in the main line of development. Yet there are a good many reasons for using the term *Homo sapiens neanderthalensis*.

The oldest genuine specimen of *Homo sapiens*—or at least of a man who very closely resembles him—was found at Swanscombe, near London, in 1935 (plate 9). A human occipital bone was unearthed seven metres deep in a gravel-pit by an amateur archaeologist. It had none of the features associated with Neanderthal man or any of his predecessors, and it resembled *Homo sapiens* in almost every respect.

Because of the surrounding soil deposits and animal bone remains, the experts were forced to the conclusion that it dated from the end of the penultimate interglacial period—that is, about 250,000 years ago.

As this bone was undamaged along the seams, it was assumed that other parts of this skull would turn up; and a year later the same archaeologist came across a left parietal-bone belonging to the same skull. For the next twenty years or so nothing was brought to light apart from nearly six hundred flint tools of the Acheulian type; however the gravel pit was reserved exclusively for diggings by archaeologists, and in 1955 the right parietal-bone was found.

In their general characteristics these skull bones—which belonged to a young woman—closely resembled their modern equivalents; as we have seen they were quite unlike those of Neanderthal man, though they were unusually thick.

Since no frontal bone has yet been found, it is not clear whether there was a ridge over the eye-sockets: however, further excavations may well bring other relics to light—and with them, one hopes, the frontal bones.

Other equally old bones illustrating the line of development to *Homo sapiens* have been found at Steinheim in Germany and at Fontéchevade in France. It would appear from all these discoveries that fundamentally *Homo sapiens* existed long before Neanderthal man: unfortunately the remains are not sufficiently complete for the picture to be quite clear.

It is strange that these men were driven out of Europe by the Neanderthalers, since when the latter died out, *Homo sapiens* reappeared in his completely modern form, that of Cro-Magnon man (plate 11).

Cro-Magnon man had a long, narrow skull, which was hardly in keeping with his low, broad face. Nobody knows as yet where he came from: some believe he originated in Asia, others in Africa. According to L. S. B. Leakey, skeletons of the Cro-Magnon type have been found in many parts of East and South Africa, but this is not a view that is shared by anybody else. The paintings on exposed rock faces which have been found in South Africa have been used as evidence that he originated there—they strikingly resemble those of East Spain—but there is little evidence to support this argument.

And just as the place of origin of Cro-Magnon man is

unresolved, so we know quite as little about where he lived once he had developed into *Homo sapiens.*

Attempts were often made to find elements of Cro-Magnon man in present-day races at the time when the superiority of certain European races was assumed: it is possible that he was a dark-skinned man, and that certain racial types related to him at that time had distinctly negroid traits. For example, certain Berber tribes in North Africa appear to have real affinities with Cro-Magnon man, as do the Guanches—the original inhabitants of the Canary Islands—who seem to have become racially mixed in spite of their being almost exterminated by the Spaniards in the fifteenth century. Their original charactersitics are still in evidence today.

The principal groups of modern man arose at the same time as Cro-Magnon man; all present-day racial features were already in evidence in him and in his various sub-divisions.

A less well-known but interesting find made as early as 1889 was that of the Javanese "Wadjak" skulls (plate 10). These people should be regarded as the forerunners of the negroid aborigines of Australia, since they have a sufficient number of features in common with them. The early aborigines originated in Java and only reached Australia in comparatively recent times, according to the latest researches.

The stone implements and artefacts of the Cro-Magnon peoples are much more varied than those of the Neanderthalers. They used bones, ivory and staghorn for the first time. In addition to the manufacture of stone and bone tools for all sorts of purposes, an artistic sense manifested itself in various forms such as scallop shell and animal tooth ornamentation. Harpoons, spears, needles and so on have been found in large numbers; in the course of time their manufacturing skills increased, as we can see from the examination of successive deposits.

It was at one time believed that Cro-Magnon man invented the bow and arrow, but it now appears unlikely that this weapon was in use until about 10,000 years ago.

The reader will realize by now that human reason and knowledge took a long time to reach maturity, and that their development was not a sudden process. Like the Neanderthalers, our prehistoric ancestors were forced by the very cold climate to live in caves and overhanging cliffs, where they were probably able to construct shelters with the aid of available branches and animal hides. Although they lived in "holes", they were certainly not primitive in either a physical or a mental sense: their brains were similar to our own, organs capable of producing the thoughts of a Plato, a Goethe or an Einstein. Their brains represented nature's most complex achievement, and were far better suited for the absorption of contemporary science than for life in a cave; perhaps the chief difference between them and ourselves is that our own minds are better exercised than theirs were.

The fantastic cave-paintings such as those found at Altamira and Lascaux were the work of Cro-Magnon man; the earliest are extremely simple and "primitive", dating from about 20,000 years ago, and they reached their highest level of development between 16,000 and 12,000 years ago. These artistic creations strikingly reveal Cro-Magnon man's urge to "reproduce" as well as the intensity of his experience, similar to those of the modern artist. These works prove that he shared the feelings and the emotions we associate with modern man; the evidence is there for all to see.

In 1940 numerous splendid paintings were discovered at Lascaux dating from the end of the Old Stone Age, as well as the remains of torches made from a resinous material mixed with animal fat, and some basin-shaped stones which had contained animal oil for lighting and had burnt black as a result.

The execution of these works of art, for that is indeed what they are, involved considerable technical difficulties; both in this respect and as regards their style they can certainly be compared with the Altamira paintings. These are usually considered the most beautiful of all, yet they began in the simplest way possible and do not look anything like as fresh and undamaged as those of Lascaux. The oldest were executed on cave walls in the form of simple scratch marks, an idea which probably originated from seeing the claw marks of bears. At a later stage paint was used: black and red only to begin with, though afterwards other colours were employed—apart, that is, from blue and green, since the processes needed for these were as yet unknown.

The exact dating of these Ice Age paintings on the basis of their style is far from simple, since crudeness of execution does not necessarily imply that they were executed at an earlier age than those of greater merit; however, in many cases a satisfactory chronological sequence based on other evidence can be provided.

These people lived as hunters and painted the pictures for reasons that had to do with fertility and hunting-magic, rather than because an excessive amount of leisure produced "art for art's sake". Evidence for this is provided by the reproduction of sexual symbols, pregnant animals or animals struck by an arrow, magicians and so on. Leroi-Gourham's researches have in fact made us realize that this whole question may be more complex than was first supposed: however, this is not the place to discuss the matter in any further detail.

Large numbers of cliff-drawings have also been found in that arid desert, the Sahara, which should remind us that the region was once very fertile and rich in river scenery: in one dried-up valley a complete fishing village has been unearthed along with heaps of shells and fishbones, and the cliff-drawings include

Fig. 10. Bison from La Grèze, near Les Eyzies (Dordogne). Etched in sharp outline only. The horns show distorted perspective and only one front and back hoof are drawn: typical of the initial (Aurignacian) period of cave art.

50

Fig. 11.   The Altamira bison in red and black (Spain).

numerous pictures of the hippopotamus and crocodile, together with representations of canoes made from reeds. All this implies that the climate of the Sahara was once warm and damp, but became arid when the last Ice Age passed away. Even in Roman times it was still possible to travel through these regions on horseback: nowadays the camel is the only animal that can be used in these areas.

We can see a slow, gradual development with regard to cave-paintings: if we look, for instance, at the La Grèze bison (near Les Eyzies in the Dordogne) we can see how the artist has produced only the outlines of his figures and without much idea of perspective (fig. 10). This engraving, which dates from the Aurignacian period about 30,000 years ago, strikes one as fairly primitive: but what a difference we notice in a similar portrait from Altamira (fig. 11) of another bison, dating this time from the end of the Magdalenian period about 12,000 years ago. This is cave-painting at its highest level of achievement; the red and black animal seems to almost speak to us from the prehistoric era, so splendidly detailed is it. Even today an artist might try hard to reproduce a living animal as well as this: and the early artist has also succeeded magnificently in conveying a sense of the creature's brute strength.

The interval of time between the two drawings mentioned is around 18,000 years—an enormous length of time, in com-

51

parison with which Christianity's centuries of growth seem insignificant. It provides an excellent example of just how slowly things developed in early prehistoric times.

We have tried to show that human evolution has been a very leisurely process, and that no acceptable explanation has yet been found which would account for the sudden and simultaneous upsurge of different cultures in many parts of the earth; and in order to get some idea of how spectacular this development was we shall examine some early civilizations in the chapters that follow—asking at the same time how it was possible that people living in the Stone Age were suddenly able to develop into cultures like those of Egypt, Troy, Crete, the Indus Valley, China and the Land of Two Rivers.

There is no chronology covering the various phases of development of, for example, prehistoric building techniques, metalworking or writing after the first burgeoning of the early civilizations. It is not surprising that virtually nothing has been published about the developments which must have had their origins (or did they?) in the Stone Age, and which were gradually improved to such an extent that at a particular time and place people were able to build pyramids after a *very* long prehistory. But archaeology fails to answer these questions.

We often read that the predynastic period or the Stone Age phase lasted until such-and-such a time—every book gives a different date!—and that immediately afterwards a particular civilization flourished; and that the same pattern occurred before the origination of every culture! But it is ridiculous that so many scientific treatises should take up the story when a culture is already in full swing, instead of starting as they ought in the Stone Age and following developments since then.

Let us take the Egyptians as an example. The ability to build pyramids demands at the least a knowledge of arithmetic, architectural techniques and skill in transporting materials—all of which suggests a long preliminary period, the existence of which is unfortunately not supported by archaeology. Archaeologists admit there is a problem here, but won't investigate the reasons for it; they simply accept the idea that the Stone Ages immediately merged into a dynastic period. And it is the same with all the other ancient civilizations; little is ever said about the prehistoric background to these civilizations, as a result of which they attempt to condense almost into insignificance a period which must have covered thousands of years between the Stone Age and the dynastic periods.

It is impossible to accept these arguments: we believe—and perhaps science, too, will come to believe—that at some stage in the very earliest period of prehistory contact was made between the ancient peoples and a still older race in possession of an advanced civilization and a history stretching a long way back indeed. It may be that there is a grain of truth in all mythological stories and legends, and that somewhere on our planet there once existed a race with a very sophisticated civilization which perished because of one or more natural disasters. The only really satisfactory theory is that the survivors of this civilization were responsible for both the technical skills and the art of writing possessed by the old cultures, who brought knowledge to the people then living in the Stone Age!

# PART TWO

# Ancient Civilization and Evolution

# Chapter Four

The prehistory of the Land of Two Rivers—where did the
Sumerians come from?—arithmetic and astronomy—the
Sumerian kings' amazing longevity—the Flood in the
Gilgamesh Epic.

Nobody denies that the Sumerians and the Land of the Two
Rivers between the Euphrates and the Tigris claim a special
place in history; but it is not as well-known that these peoples
also had a prehistory.

Long before the Sumerians arrived the Land of the Two
Rivers was inhabited, and although skeletal remains are none
too plentiful in this area, we know how these peoples of the
prehistoric era lived from the different types of Old and New
Stone Age tools and so forth which have been found. These
indicate a gradual development from the most primitive types
of stone tool, and although those dating from the earliest period
are fewer in number than in other parts of the Mediterranean
regions it would be mistaken to regard them as some kind of
curiosity, as repeatedly asserted both in scientific and non-
scientific literature on the subject.

It is often forgotten that it is not the quantities of sites or
objects found in sites which matter when one is trying to trace a
line of development. Writers often use such terms as "primitive
man", "savages", "half-savages", "primitive apes", "half-apes"
and so on to describe *Homo sapiens* or a direct forerunner of his,
yet these people were not primitive in a bodily sense—which in
some people seems to arouse a certain *Angst*—but only as far as
culture, religion and so forth are concerned.

An extremely common and widespread misconception is that
many different races met together in the Land of Two Rivers,
a misconception that originated in the multiplicity of styles

represented in their surviving images and figurines, which are held to indicate a jumble of different races with differing physiognomical traits. In reality, however, only two clearly different physical types occur in Sumerian–Accadian times, one of which has a sharply protuberant nose, a backwards arching forehead and a flat occiput, while the other has a round face and a straight nose.

The oldest human remains in the region are the Neanderthal skeletons from the Shanidar cave—certainly a primitive type, but not merely so primitive or strange as the better-known Neanderthalers of Western Europe. The remains of seven adults and the heavily damaged skull of a child were found in cave deposits five metres thick—layers of rubble had collected in the course of about 100,000 years, and these were dated by means of the Carbon 14 method. A sample from the second stratum (B) was about 12,000 years old; another from layer C was about 29,000 years old, and yet another (from C) from a depth of four and a half metres was over 34,000 years old; but since this method can become very untrustworthy if continued too far, the age of the oldest deposit was assumed to be around 44,000 years while the child's skull, although badly damaged, was probably about 70,000 years old, which means that the Shanidar cave was presumably inhabited for about 60,000 years by Neanderthalers, a period of something like two thousand generations.

In another and more recent deposit from the same cave relics of a new culture known as the Baradostian were found, which show some affinities with those of Cro-Magnon man in Europe; in fact they may well have been contemporaneous.

In this culture bone-working was much less developed than it was in Europe, which again suggests that there was enough hardwood available instead as a result of a cooler climatic phase.

On the whole the Land of Two Rivers shows a very gradual development, quite different from the sudden flourishing of Sumerian civilization. Even the site of Jarmo, which with some justice has been described as the oldest village in the Middle East, gives us no clue to the sudden and simultaneous appearance of the civilizations of the Mediterranean regions and the Land of Two Rivers. In Jarmo the remains of houses were found in fifteen successive deposits, the lowest of which provided no earthenware artefacts, since the first inhabitants were stone-using herdsmen. The transition from food-gathering to food-producing seems to have taken place here between 5000 and 4500 B.C.

What is known of the Sumerians? Only that they appear in Southern Mesopotamia somewhere between the sixth and fourth millennia B.C., presumably from the east—though where they came from is unknown. It was they who left the ziggurats, sacred domes dedicated to the moon-god Nana, in one of which Sir Leonard Woolley came across an ingenious drainage system complete with pipes very like those of Crete and Egypt, and even resembling those of ancient America.

But it is not just the ziggurats and the drainage systems which deserve our attention; everything suggests that the cultural level was truly high. This was a civilization with a writing-system; its initial pictograms developed later into the so-called "cunei-form" style. The pictorial form of writing must have existed though there are scarcely any samples of it left, thanks to the perishable nature of the material; on the other hand clay tablets have been found in large numbers. An afterlife was certainly believed in, since the grave-goods were clearly meant for the dead man's use; and Sir Leonard Woolley also found among these some beautifully worked artefacts revealing a high level of artistic expression and technique.

Apart from the still unsolved problem of their origin, there is also the question of how the Sumerians managed to bring their culture to such a pitch of development, which—relatively speaking—occurred quite shortly after their arrival in Mesopotamia. To take their writing alone as an example: how many hundreds or even thousands of years must it have taken to evolve any pictorial writing, and subsequently cuneiform writing? The sheer problems involved in making it suitable for complicated calculations or complex administrations must have been for-midable. At first sight it seems unlikely that such a development could have taken place in Mesopotamia itself: but what was the origin of their knowledge, every aspect of which implies a long growth and maturation? Whatever facet of their culture one likes to consider, whether it be their mathematics, their building techniques—which even to us seem extraordinarily skilful—their religious rites or their metal-working, the evidence seems to indicate an *extremely* long incubation period!

But one must be careful, for it is just this kind of history and gradual development that the Sumerians could *not* have had! Remember what science tells us: that somewhere between the sixth and fourth millennia the Sumerians arrived in Mesopotamia.

There is no evidence of their having possessed an advanced civilization before they settled there, and so one has to assume that it developed solely in Mesopotamia. But this is chronologically impossible! How could hunters, nomads and simple farmers have traversed within a relatively short time-span all the stages of development required to make of them experienced builders, metal-workers and artists? Remember, too, the religious rites, and particularly the writing, which alone needs an enormous length of time in which to develop.

In the opening chapters emphasis was laid on the gradualness of human evolution, perhaps best illustrated by the bison drawings with an eighteen thousand-year gap between them: so it is reasonable to ask how long evolution from Stone Age conditions to a level comparable with that of Mesopotamia *must* have taken. It must have lasted far longer than the two thousand years which people would have us believe.

The degree of Sumerian civilization became apparent after they had been conquered by the barbarian semitic tribes of the Babylonians and Assyrians, who were unrelated to the peoples of Sumeria. The Babylonians built up their own civilization on the foundations laid by the Sumerians to an extent and a depth which must be acknowledged by anyone studying the history of these races. Perhaps it would be more correct to say that the conquerors were themselves conquered, since despite their physical and military strength, the Babylonians could not inhibit the survival or indeed the further development of the earlier culture.

The extent of Mesopotamian influence on other races was demonstrated by the excavation in 1853 of the library of the Assyrian king Ashurbanipal the First (668–626 B.C.) at Nineveh. It was only in 1872 that experts managed to decipher the texts on the clay tablets found there, which contained among other things the now world-famous Gilgamesh epic, together with the story of *the* Flood. We stress the word "the" because it is impossible to believe that this account, made long before the time of Christ, so closely resembles the version given in the Bible merely by chance! And early in this century other texts were brought to light which were connected with this story and had been written 2500 years B.C. The hero of the Gilgamesh epic listens to the following story from one Uta-Napishtim:

"The mighty gods, according to Uta-Napishtim, were gathered together and looked down upon Earth and were filled with wrath at the wickedness of men's ways. So they decided upon the total destruction of mankind and thus brought about a great Flood to sweep away every man, woman and child from the face of the Earth. But in the assembly of gods there was Ea, Uta-Napishtim's beloved, who warned her loved one of the disaster to come, commanding him to build a ship of six decks and to take on board his sons and women and all the animals of the field and all cattle thereof. Uta-Napishtim followed her counsel and after he had built the ship and had gone on board dark clouds filled the heavens and the rains began to descend in torrents. For six days and nights the tempest raged and when after this he looked out he beheld an endless sea covering the surface of the world as far as the eye could reach.

"After seven days the peak of a mountain arose upon which the ship remained fast. Thereupon Uta-Napishtim set free a dove which however returned unto him, not finding any place to settle. A swallow did likewise but finally on the third day a crow departed from the ship and did not return because she had found some sustenance."

This ancient story is merely one of many found on the tablets, which include that of Paradise and of Adam and Eve. Of course there are differences: Adam and Eve have different names, and the serpent is a fox, but otherwise the story is just like our Genesis version.

Incidentally George Smith's decipherment of these texts caused a storm of protest among Christians, perhaps because it showed that the Bible contained a story which was already 2500 years old and had come from Mesopotamia.

In the Mesopotamian area as well as in other sites of the Mediterranean regions mud deposits two or three metres thick have been found, demonstrating indisputably that at one time prolonged and extensive inundations had indeed taken place: however the problem here is one of dating. From what period of Mesopotamian history does the story derive, and who wrote it? Does the story of the Flood refer to the mud deposits of both Mesopotamia and the Mediterranean, or was it merely one of several such floods the world has known? And must we look still further back in time for an explanation?

The most important question concerns the identity of the people who brought civilization to the Land of Two Rivers. As far as Mesopotamia is concerned, there are still a good many questions to which Von Daniken and others think they can provide the answers by pointing to extraterrestrial causes.

As we have seen, Von Daniken sees man as the end-product of an extraterrestrial power which intervened in the process of evolution at an unknown date, This theory is one we can and would wish to refute. We agree with him that a solution to the problem of sudden and simultaneous cultural developments must be found, and it is natural that having found no scientific explanation in the conditions on our own planet he should look for an explanation in space. The difficulties certainly exist, but we feel we can find terrestrial solutions to them.

Although we greatly admire new and revolutionary ideas such

as those proposed by Von Daniken, we would like to test them against our own beliefs; by the end of this book two different versions of a limited number of discoveries and curiosities will have been put forward, and we leave it to the reader to decide which of the two he prefers: what now follows should not be taken as an attack upon Von Daniken, but rather as a fresh interpretation based on the discoveries already made.

The widely discussed and almost unbelievably sophisticated Sumerian astronomy was actually Babylonian, since although the Sumerians studied the skies and named the star-formations, this could hardly be described as astronomy; it was instead a form of astrology, since their religious festivals and the important events of their daily life corresponded with the movements of the heavens. Similarly when the Mesopotamians ascertained the exact orbit of the moon around 500 B.C., this was in fact essentially a Babylonian achievement; and proper scientific observations only began about two hundred years after this.

A writer called Pieter Coll, who is opposed to Von Daniken, asserts in his book *Hebben zij Gelijk* that the horns of Venus were observed as early as 4000 years ago, an assumption he bases on a Sumerian cylindrical barrel seal. He tries to prove this by reference to an image of the king Urnammu in which he claims that Venus is outlined; but in fact it represents the more easily observable crescent moon, which also appears in the picture of King Melishipak the Second and many others from the Land of Two Rivers. The moon-god was the most important deity to the Babylonians until quite late times, whereas in every Mesopotamian culture the planet Venus has always been shown as a star rather than as crescent. There is no evidence for the claim that Venus could have been observed by Chaldean astronomers through telescopes, and the interpretation of the crescent moon and other sacred symbols is at fault. Certainly there are in existence clay tablets about 4000 years old which describe the movements of Venus, but the phases of this planet had definitely not been discovered as early as that.

The same writer finds it surprising that the Chaldeans already seemed to know about the planet Uranus, and he finds it equally amazing that they should have known that Mars has two moons of its own. This would seem to imply that their astronomers possessed ultra-modern telescopes; yet has any evidence for this far-fetched theory ever been found? We are prepared to admit that they used such instruments as soon as it can be *proved* in any way.

In the Louvre there is a milestone from the reign of King Melishipak the Second (also known as Melishkon); examples of these are known from various centuries, but they originated among the Kassites. They are in fact boundary-stones, used initially on estates but later stored in temple archives as proofs of the ownership of land. This stone clearly shows the goddess Nana receiving King Melishipak and his daughter (plate 12). The symbols shown are those of Ishtar (the goddess of the morning and evening star Venus), Sin (the moon-god) and Shamash (sub-god).

The meanings attached to these divinities are as follows: Ishtar (Astarte, Ashera) was the goddess of love; Sin is

Fig. 12. Three drawings of the "winged sun-ship" and one of Von Daniken's "aeroplane".

the moon-god illuminating the path of the nomads across the Steppes, and Shamash is the sun-god, the protector of the oppressed who searches for injustices in all the dark corners of the world in his daily journey across the sky.

The milestone symbols occur in a vast number of cases on similar reliefs and inscriptions; and although their significance is fully known, partly through the accompanying texts on the clay tablets, they are nonetheless employed by writers to prove the existence of astronomy among the Sumerians.

The diagram of the "flying machine" (fig. 12) must also be considered: this was found on one of the cylinder seals from the library of Ashurbanipal, and certainly looks somewhat like a stylized version of an aircraft. It seems more likely, however, that it represents part of the epic era of Irra, the god of plagues, and though when seen beside the other sacred symbols it is possible to make out its supposedly "aeronautical" lines, it is in fact a symbol of the winged sun-ship which in a less stylized form occurs frequently on other Babylonian artefacts. The same symbol can be seen on the British Museum's famous black obelisk of Salmanassar the Third, where the sun-ship is even more clearly delineated: and it can often be found in Persia as well, especially in conjunction with the god Ahuramazda.

* * *

Another subject well worth studying is Babylonian—and not Sumerian—mathematics. A great deal is talked about their elaborate calculations, though there is nothing really all that unusual about them. They based their work on an enumeration-system using sixty as a unit, by which means very large numbers could be expressed by the use of very few digits. Our own system is based on tens, and we would need a row of fifteen figures to express numbers for which the Babylonians only used eight Nevertheless their system was not free of faults, since they had no zero and no commas; with the result that sometimes the actual numbers meant by the Babylonians when they wrote them down could only be understood by referring to the accompanying figures or calculations. It was not until about

200 B.C. that a symbol was invented for use as a zero between two figures.

Incidentally, the ancient Greeks also had their mathematical problems, since even at the height of their civilization they were unable to express numbers greater than 10,000, anything above that figure being considered "infinite". It was only later in their history that this system was replaced: the number 10,000 was of course still used, or rather the symbol indicating it, but for numbers greater than 10,000 they placed above it a letter showing the factor by which 10,000 was to be multiplied. All the same the system was too complex for daily needs, so they resorted to a kind of counting-frame from which the figures were read off vertically. It is remarkable that the Greeks applied the idea (as we ourselves do) of the place-value of figures perfectly, but were not successful in substituting written signs for this process.

*     *     *

A further subject which is open to varying interpretations is the fantastic longevity of the Sumerian kings, which can be demonstrated by putting together all the various dynasties and their kings—an enormous time-span. Determining their ages is rather like the problem of Methuselah and his 969 years: the twenty-three kings who reigned in the Land of Two Rivers after the Flood ruled altogether for more than 24,000 years. In Kish there appear to have been twelve dynasties totalling fifty-six kings who supposedly reigned for more than seven thousand years in all, and followed the already-mentioned mythological kings. But here again it should be pointed out that there is no contemporary evidence to prove this, and none at all from the excavations in the royal city of Kish to show that any of the twenty-three kings even existed; they probably ought to be classified as mythological beings, along with their lengthy reigns.

One could get the impression that each of these kings reigned in turn, but from excavations and other evidence it has been established that they were all merely princes of cities with very limited powers, so that to place these dynasties in succession is

quite misleading: in fact those princes who achieved indepen-
dence must have been named together and not one after another.

We are still left with the important problem of where the
Sumerians came from and how early civilization originated
there. How and from whom did they obtain their specialized
knowledge?

# Chapter Five

Agriculture, trade and shipping in Ancient Egypt—how were the Pyramids built?—the riddle of the empty sarcophagi and the vanished mummies—ancient Egyptian mathematics and the measurements of the Cheops pyramid —an almost fatal error in construction!

The ancient civilization of Egypt is one of the best known of all; experts have been able to build up an exact picture of what life must have been like because so many artefacts have been left behind.

One of the most important requirements for the development of an advanced civilization was met very early on in Egypt, namely, an abundance of food. Extensive researches have shown that the first inhabitants of the Nile delta cultivated barley and wheat in the fertile mud in the pre-dynastic period around 3800–3600 B.C., and very probably much earlier. We have recovered wooden sickles with flint blades, hand-mills and flails together with the remains of granaries from the Fayum A period (*circa* 5000 B.C.) in southern Deir Tasa and northern Merimde.

Some writers on the subject are doubtful about using the word agriculture in this connection since they feel that the earliest Egyptians did not possess other than the crudest farming techniques, but the facts contradict this view. There was no need to employ more sophisticated agricultural methods, since it was merely a question of sowing in the rich mud and then harvesting, and the growing was left to nature.

But the Egyptians had an eye for improvements; in the reign of Pharaoh Mena or Menes (*circa* 3200 B.C.) extensive irrigation works were built in the Nile delta which were later enlarged and perfected. Even the Sumerians adopted some of their techniques of irrigation.

King Scorpion's so-called "club-head", which is in the Ashmolean Museum at Oxford, comes from approximately the same period. It was found at Hierakonpolis and is estimated to be about 5200 years old. On its surface (plate 13) one can see an agricultural rite is clearly depicted, palpable proof that the Egyptians were already versed in farming over 5000 years ago!

There is even clearer evidence of trade and shipping; copper ore occurs in small quantities in Egypt but there is hardly enough for commercial exploitation, which means that they were therefore very dependent on imports. In the late pre-dynastic period (about 3400–3200 B.C.), and probably earlier, the Egyptians were trading with Sinai and places in the Arabian deserts where copper was available in considerable quantities; and from this time on copper was used for the manufacture of weapons and tools, though stone implements were still in use and remained so for a fairly long time. And the discovery of copper pins and soapstone beads at Badari and El Amra provides conclusive evidence of contact with other advanced cultures at an even earlier period (4000–3600 B.C.).

The best proof of this trade is furnished by the small cylinder seals made of stone, ivory or other material which were decorated in such a way as to be suitable for the sole use of individual magistrates and merchants. They were rather like our own hallmarks and, as the name suggests, they were rolled over wet clay rather than pressed into it. Some of these cylinder seals clearly show Mesopotamian origin, and they have also been found in a Gerzian tomb at Negada.

One of the most interesting discoveries from the same period is a flint-stone knife with an ivory handle (plates 14 and 15), which was recovered at Gebel el Arak and is now in the Louvre in Paris. One side clearly shows a Mesopotamian hero conquering two lions, while on the other, more interesting side two rows of ships can be seen: the top line of which are typical of the Tigris "Belem", while the lower line are Egyptian ships of the Gerza period (*circa* 3500 B.C.). The same theme is also to be found on an Egyptian tomb painting in Hierakonpolis, which is about 5500 years on.

But one of the clearest proofs that there was shipping at so early a period comes from a mastaba in Sakkara, which is ascribed to King Djet, a First Dynasty prince flourishing around 3200–2900 B.C.

Still more dramatically the archaeologist Emery unearthed a pit roofed with large stone slabs which contained a boat in two parts which, when reassembled, was about forty-three metres long! The boat is now being restored under the direction of the Egyptian archaeologist Ahmed Youssef. Aerial photography shows that there are more of these pits in the same area waiting to be opened! Recently the well-decks of boats have been found on all four approaches to the Cheops pyramid.

Finally, we have dozens if not hundreds of pictures of Egyptian ships, of which the most typical and striking are those in the temple of Queen Hatshepsut. Among other things the legendary voyage of discovery to the land of Punt is depicted, along with pictures of perfectly sea-worthy ships.

But despite all this evidence there are still questions that need to be answered. During the reconstruction of the boat discovered by Emery it became clear how very elegant it was, perhaps even more attractive than the craft built by the Vikings thousands of years later. The hull was beautifully streamlined, and the stern was high and graceful. But the remarkable thing was that, despite external appearances—and in contrast to the Viking ships— these vessels were not at all sea-worthy! They were not reinforced in such a way as to prevent them collapsing in heavy seas, and yet they must have been used for a considerable length of time because the boarding had been worn down by the ropes in places. Everything suggests that although they looked sea-worthy, these vessels were only meant for use on the Nile, which is always calm: at sea the first waves would have destroyed them. But how can we explain their sea-going appearance if they were intended solely for the Nile? Did the Egyptians have contacts with some other race capable of building sea-going ships?

It seems unlikely that the Egyptians, who in nearly every other respect showed so much technical insight, would have borrowed only the external appearance of such ships: some other factor must lie behind this state of affairs.

If one inspects old papyrus boats one notices at once the same streamlined hull and the height of bows and stern; and these were vessels that also lacked ribs and other forms of reinforcement. If one then compares an ancient Egyptian river-craft with a papyrus boat it seems almost certain that the latter must have been the model for the former at a time when the Egyptians had no knowledge or experience of timber ships. We stress the word timber because the enormous sea-going potential of the papyrus boat has been proved by Thor Heyerdahl's famous Ra voyages. Heyerdahl has the distinction of being the first man to realize the potential of this type of craft, and his journey across the Atlantic showed that the Egyptians were certainly not limited to the Nile or to the Mediterranean Sea.

After reading his report and studying his plan of construction we believe that Heyerdahl made just one mistake. Time after time during the journey Ra's steering oars broke, and even in calm weather they seemed unable to cope with the force of water without breaking off. Heyerdahl and Bjorn Landstrom used copies of countless ancient reliefs for their building plans; Ra was perfectly seaworthy apart from the steering gear, which was really only suitable for the Nile. From the plan (fig. 13) it can be seen that the oars were fastened at two points, which meant that it was impossible to absorb the force of the waves except to the extent of the elasticity of the wood itself, and naturally this was not enough. On his second journey Heyerdahl tried using much heavier steering oars but following the same construction; these, too, broke off like matchsticks in the slightest sea, despite their being almost as thick as telegraph poles. Moreover the oar blades were vertical in the water, and in this respect he was again following ancient Egyptian drawings. It may be that Heyerdahl did not realize that the Egyptians did not portray things very exactly in their sketches—for example, profile outlines of the human figure were executed in such a way that both shoulders, as well as the body, could be seen. Similarly with the oars: the artists wanted to show both of them and so drew them

71

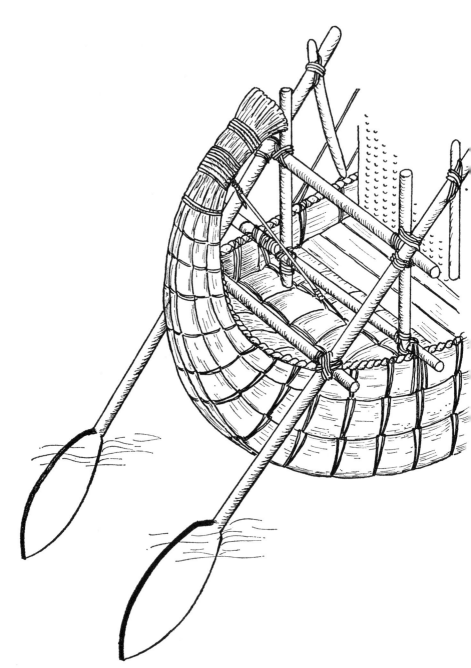

Fig. 13. The oars are fixed at two places and therefore cannot turn. Furthermore the blades are vertical in the water, not horizontal—so things must go wrong!

Fig. 14. The Egyptians drew the whole oar as if it were vertical in the water during the journey; but this was not in fact the case. This sketch shows that the oars were fixed at one point and can thus turn, in contrast to the steering mechanism which Heyerdahl used for his Ra papyrus boat.

as if they were vertical in the water (fig. 14), but this does not necessarily mean that during a voyage both oars were kept in this position!

Later ships designed for trading by sea show quite clearly that the oars were not fastened in two places but in one only, with the result that they could turn (fig. 15). When both oars were placed flat on the water on either side of the boat it was only necessary to pull one up and let the other go deeper into the water to make the ship turn quickly to starboard or port; using a simple model, we succeeded perfectly in making the little vessel turn quickly either way. In the open sea this would also have the advantage of allowing the oars to ride over heavy waves,

Fig. 15. It must have been like this, with the oars flat in the water and hinged at only one point.

in line with the papyrus boat principle of counteracting the waves; it was only in this way that the oars could turn without snapping off. An even more efficient form of steering was the diamond-shaped oar, which offered less resistance to the water but retained the good steering potential.

It was only necessary to fix the oars in a certain position if one wanted to follow a definite course—with no risk of their breaking. There may have been a second fastening—seen on the drawing as a sort of helm—which would have allowed considerable free play if, for example, it were a rope fixture, and would have withstood the force of quite heavy seas.

In time the Egyptians became excellent sailors; so what is the explanation of the high fore and aft of the papyrus boats? The answer is that if one had struck sail and the oars were vertical in the water, at sea in a heavy storm they would have acted as a sort of drift-anchor and forced the boat around so that the stern was pointing in the direction in which it had been sailing. Here again we can see how they must have built up their knowledge of both papyrus and wooden boats through their experiences, since both types were in fact suitable for the open sea! They evolved a somewhat appealing system to prevent shipwreck: a hawser lay over the whole length of the boat which was fixed both fore and aft by a loop. If there was any play in the hawser it could be tightened by means of a wooden spoke, thus ensuring that the naturally flexible hull stayed taut and resilient. This ingenious system was perhaps employed first on papyrus vessels, and it meant that frail river craft could at last be transformed into proper wooden sea-going ships!

*　　*　　*

We must now examine the way in which the pyramids were built and how the stone-work was dressed, a subject that is still a mystery to many people; and we can see how the ancient Egyptians literally moved mountains through their technical skills and the fairly simple means at their disposal.

In the older history books one reads that the Egyptians merely used wedges of copper and wood to dislodge the stone from the rock-faces; yet it seems hard to believe that they could have achieved this by such methods. The truth of the matter was rather different. They did use wooden wedges (which on being made wet expanded and so cracked the rock) and copper ones as well; but they also had bronze and copper saws, together with other instruments. This metal was too soft for stone-working purposes, but they found that if a quantity of quartz sand was

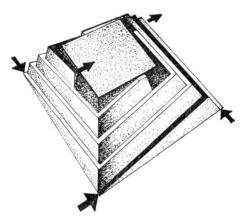

Fig. 16. The great blocks of stone were transported up the pyramid in this manner and materials no longer needed were brought down again.

added during the smelting, it turned almost as hard as diamond. There is also some evidence that copper and bronze implements were sharpened with topaz, beryl and sapphire.

The stones were transported either by ship or overland by means of wooden rollers and sledges—the same method used by the Italian archaeologist Giovanni Belzoni around 1810 to transport to the banks of the Nile the gigantic head of the statue of Rameses the Second, which is now in the British Museum.

It is often claimed that we do not know exactly how the pyramids were constructed; but an extremely convincing explanation has been provided by the American archaeologist Dows Dunham.

The Egyptians made use of four channels, which ran obliquely from the four corners of the pyramid to the top, and while three of them were used to transport stone and other material upwards, the fourth was used for carrying the stone-waste down again (fig. 16). Examples of the use of these paths or channels can be seen on Mycerinus, the smallest of the three pyramids of Giza, and on the unfinished Sechim-chet, which is estimated to have an area of 120 × 120 metres. In both these cases the remains of the channels have been found.

The building of a pyramid is often depicted as an arduous process of piling stones on top of each other, yet it would be more reasonable to think in terms of a continuous stream of groups of labourers (about fifteen to twenty-five for each block of stone) dragging the stones to the top along the channels by means of wooden rollers and/or sledges.

Although it is often said that the work took centuries, it is more likely that the construction time was, in fact, appreciably shorter because of the methods used. Experts estimate the number of actual workers involved in building a pyramid to be between 2500 and 4000 men, rather than the hundreds of thousands sometimes suggested; although the pyramids have large surfaces, there would not have been enough room for such a number to stand, let alone work!

A recently published theory claimed that there was no shortage of workers to build the pyramids, since many farm-workers willingly offered their services for this purpose when unemployed by the flooding of the Nile: but as yet there is not enough evidence to prove it.

Equally fanciful are the estimates for population of the Nile delta at the time when these first pyramids were built: some say five million, others fifty million, and still others around one hundred million. But bear in mind that Holland has about thirteen million inhabitants living in a space two to three times the size of the regions of the Nile valley which were inhabited at that time: how could there possibly have been room for fifty or even a hundred million people?

Another problem facing some writers is that empty graves and sarcophagi have been unearthed during excavations; these have sometimes been approached in a rather "mystical" way, yet there is nothing strange or mystical about them when they are examined more closely. Mention is often made of Doctor

77

Goneim, who in 1954 came across an empty sarcophagus at Sakkara in the course of his archaeological work: and of the young archaeologist Emil Brugsch, who began investigating a warren of hidden corridors and rooms in the Valley of the Kings on the strength of an account by one Abd el-Rasoel, and found no less than forty coffins, including those containing the remains of Thutmoses the Third, Rameses the Second and Seti the First. These coffins were in a chaotic state but were accompanied by grave-goods; everything suggested that this was not a normal, orderly burial. The problem was solved by a papyrus from the time of Rameses the Ninth, from which it appeared that almost immediately after the pharaoh's funeral it was feared that it might fall victim to tomb-robbers. Almost the only defence against the robbers was to transfer the mummy or mummies and most of the grave-goods elsewhere as soon as the priests received reports of an impending attack; and if an attack had already been made on a tomb elsewhere the process of opening it would naturally have taken a day or two, which would have given the priests time to accomplish their tasks—otherwise Emil Brugsch would never have made his discoveries. Several mummies were found in other places which were not their original burial-sites. Incidentally, the punishment of tomb-robbers was often portrayed in wall paintings and in stone especially under the last of the pharaohs.

The sarcophagi were also emptied of their contents for quite a different reason, which was that throughout the following centuries the delicately painted mummies were used a great deal for medical purposes: an example being the English trader who shipped away a whole consignment of them in 1586 in the belief that they were especially effective in the treatment of "phthisis, all kinds of debility and digestive disturbances".

*     *     *

Another subject which fascinated many people for a number of years was Egyptian mathematics, which when applied to the pyramids gave dimensions revealing all kinds of strange affinities. Here we must literally cite Von Daniken and Charroux, the most modern of the arithmeticians concerned with the pyramids:

"Is it really due to chance," Von Daniken writes in his book *Was God an Astronaut?*, "that the height of the Cheops pyramid when multiplied by one milliard (1,000,000,000) tallies with the distance between Earth and Sun and that the area of the pyramid when divided by twice the height [N.B. Why exactly twice?] should give us the famous pi (3·1416)?"

It is worth looking into these claims in some detail. In the first place, it is particularly difficult to estimate even roughly the height or area of a pyramid since they have unfortunately crumbled and weathered so much in the course of time; so one can find the original dimensions only within certain limits. This means that if the height is multiplied by 1,000,000,000 considerable disparities will arise between the different estimates, and the resultant figures are unlikely to correspond convincingly to the distance between the earth and the sun; on top of which, this distance itself changes because of the earth's weak elliptical orbit, so that one can really only talk about an average distance.

In his book, *The Unknown Past*, Charroux sets out a different multiplication: the height of the pyramid (148·208 metres?) multiplied by a million gives, approximately, a figure similar to the distance of the earth from the sun. But let us calculate: 1,000,000 × 148·208 *metres* = 148,208 kilometres! But the average distance is 149,600,000 kilometres, which thus means a difference of around 149,000,000 kilometres!

So much for our pyramid calculators, The Egyptians are credited with advanced arithmetical abilities but this, too, we will leave to the reader to decide. Whenever the Egyptians multiplied figures it was carried out by addition. Taking 18 × 6 as an example: they kept adding 18 and inserting the figure 1 alongside each 18, putting it on the right; and when this 1 occurred in the total 6×, one knew that the result of the process could be found in the left-hand column. The tabulation of this is shown on the following page. As you see, it was a very cumbersome procedure.

| 18 | 1 |
| 18 | 1 |
| — | |
| 36 | |
| 18 | 1 |
| — | |
| 54 | |
| 18 | 1 |
| — | |
| 72 | |
| 18 | 1 |
| — | |
| 90 | |
| 18 | 1 |
| — | — |
| 108 | 6 |

Much the same system was used for division, but the idea of fractions caused the Egyptians almost insuperable difficulties. Since they only had the numerator 1, they had to express, say, the fraction $\frac{7}{12}$ as $\frac{1}{3} + \frac{1}{6} + \frac{1}{12}$. In general, therefore, we may safely suppose from these examples that the Egyptians never really searched for the principles of arithmetic. To ask about the whys and wherefores of things was too much to expect from such a practically minded people; all that the Egyptians needed were methods for calculating quantities of food, areas of land, the levels of the Nile and so forth.

In geometry, however, they did achieve something, since they managed to calculate areas of triangles, rectangles and other such figures: even the volume of a pyramid was assessed with a reasonable accuracy, as well as the value of pi at 3·16.

In order to fix the Nile levels the Egyptians introduced a calendar based on the rising of the Dog Star Syrius, which shone brightly every 365 days, coinciding approximately with the annual flooding of the Nile; and this provides a good illustration of the practical turn of their minds.

\*      \*      \*

Innumerable books, scientific and unscientific, have been written on the subject of Egypt, and anyone who studies them can hardly fail to notice a pattern running through them. They tend to begin with a discussion of Egypt's prehistoric period, which often takes up little more than a page or two, after which attention is immediately transferred to the builders of the pyramids. Great emphasis is laid on knowledge of the dynastic Egyptians, and it is frequently suggested that Mesopotamia and Egypt, in particular, mutually influenced each other. But most of these volumes—which are often filled with splendid photographs and sketches—are essentially concerned with sifting through and categorizing the discoveries that have been made with a view to reconstructing Egyptian history; and one of the unpleasant consequences of the increasingly specialized nature of archaeology, every branch of which has its own experts today, is that people with a more general vision and knowledge are growing steadily scarcer. This may be the reason why people seldom ask for any proof of there having been a *gradual transition* from the Stone Age to the age of the pyramids.

Such proof does not exist. The archaeologists can produce evidence of the evolution of writing, metal-working, ship-building, architecture and numerous other matters between these two periods. As relative "laymen" rather than as scientists, we have realized that there must be some solution to the question of how Egyptian civilization came into being!

Science tries to provide an answer in a gradual growth which did *not* exist. One of the strongest arguments against this theory lies in the sheer variety of peoples involved, peoples who were often not related to each other in any respect whatsoever—quite apart from which they were often separated from each other by immense distances. It is only if we take one and the same race and spread them over the various parts of the world, at the same time assuming a favourable climate and an identical stage of development, that a simultaneous flourishing of cultures becomes explicable. Nor should the settings for these civilizations be too different from place to place: yet, if we look at the places where the ancient cultures developed—Mesopotamia, Egypt,

China, the regions around the Indus, Crete and Troy—we in fact see great differences between them. These are areas which were inhabited by peoples who were not related, and they are separated from each other by natural obstacles! Was this a case of a simultaneous upsurge of cultures, each marking a transition from the Stone Age—a transition just as big as that we are making today into the age of space-travel?

Opponents of this view will point at once to the different dates of origin of the old civilizations; but how great are these differences in fact? A thousand years? Two thousand years? Almost certainly: but even then the problem remains, for how significant is a period of one, two or even three thousand years beside the many tens of thousands, or for that matter hundreds of thousands of years man had already existed prior to this?

As we have seen, it took 18,000 years to progress from a drawing of a bison consisting solely of outlines without any perspective to one that was full of detail and almost perfect technically; and the development of hand-axes, spears, clubs and other weapons and implements suggests a very slow process of growth completely at variance with the idea that the ancient civilizations suddenly came into being. To suggest a "rapid" transition from the Stone Age to the ancient civilizations is, chronologically speaking, quite absurd! The inhabitants of those areas where civilizations arose and flourished *must*, quite simply, have made contact with another race—whom we shall term the Ancients—who already possessed a fairly high level of sophistication at that time. Did this race belong to our own world or were they cosmonauts?

# Chapter Six

The Bible and evolution—was Darwin the first evolution-
ist?—which story of the Creation is correct?—is man a
mammal?—the theory of evolution and its foundations—
the Ark of the Covenant—can man create life artificially?

It is well-known that the Bible should not be taken as a reliable
guide to natural history or as a scientific treatise, and on closer
inspection there is plenty of evidence to support this point of
view. The first doubts about the dependability of the Bible appeared when it was realized that the world is a sphere, and that
the sun does not revolve around it, but vice versa: whereas the
compilers of the Bible proceeded from the assumption that the
Earth was a flat disc supported on columns (Job, chapter 38).

Today we all take it for granted that this is not so, and accept
that the world revolves around the sun. In order to accept the
findings of modern science we have had to give up many of the
beliefs held by the original writers of the Bible, with the result
that the Bible is no longer taken literally—at least as far as the
natural sciences are concerned.

Although the Book of Genesis was one of the last books of
the Old Testament to be written, the story of the Creation was
inevitably influenced by the unscientific ideas held at the time
about the origin and development of life. Yet it is not true to say
that the idea of evolution is entirely modern, originating in the
work of Darwin; the ancient Greeks were very interested in the
origins of things, and whether the chicken or the egg came first.

As early as the sixth century B.C. Thales was saying that water
was the "mother" of all things, while Heraclitus had declared
that every living creature was always changing into new forms.
In the fifth century B.C. the Greek philosopher Empedocles
(493–435 B.C.) thought that life arose spontaneously, and that

organisms developed slowly after numerous failures; in this respect he came very close to Darwin's theory of the survival of the fittest.

Aristotle (384–322 B.C.) argued lucidly that there was a natural transition from plant to animal and that man was the apex of a straight linear development. Scientists in ancient times thought in terms of logic and abstract theories, and considered practical research to be unnecessary; but an attempt was made to solve the problem of how forms of life arose by using examples provided by nature. They confined themselves to dealing with superficial characteristics only, because of the over-abundance and the sheer complexity of species that could be studied. It was held that the legless animals were the first group to have arisen on earth—the teeming creatures of the sea and the fish of the oceans; the next stage was thought to be represented by the birds, whereas those animals with four (or more) limbs—mammals, limbed reptilia and so forth—came later. The first book of Genesis builds up the story of Creation on the basis of this order.

It is known from anatomical, palaeontological and other biological evidence that the many-limbed insects belong to the primitive invertebrate animals, that amphibians developed after fish; and that birds and mammals subsequently split off from the reptiles. Quite a different version of the Creation is given in the second book of Genesis to that appearing in the first book. In this second account much more reference is made to Sumerian and Babylonian stories of the Creation: practically the whole of the first eleven chapters of Genesis derives from the folk-lore and mythologies of these civilizations, and one comes across other of their myths and legends, or fragments of them, elsewhere in the Bible in verse and narrative.

In this second Creation story no mention is made of the days it took for God to make the world; it is already in being, and the story tells us of the creation of man, followed by the founding of the Garden of Eden. Animals and birds appear next—there is no mention of fish—while woman is formed last of all.

Thus we have here two contradictory versions, the first of which introduces man and woman at the end of the story while the second begins with the male, introduces the animals and mentions woman last.

According to various Mesopotamian stories of the Creation man is made of clay—in fact the Hebrew word for "making" is the same as that used for the activities of the potter—and Genesis Book One uses this, while the Creation story as found in Job 38 (which is very different from the two Genesis accounts) suggests affinities with the Accadian version. The details given in Psalm 74 concerning the Creation also agree very closely with this Accadian one, which tells how Marduk, the supreme god, is killed by Tiamat, a seven-headed monster. In Psalm 74 this creature is called Leviathan, which is the same as the Ugaritic Lotan, the dragon killed by Baal. There are many other places in the Bible where mention is made of the dragon Leviathan during the Creation.

Even if we leave aside other accounts of Creation, one of these two fundamentally different accounts from Genesis must have been thought of as inaccurate even at a time when people believed in the literal truth of the Bible as far as real events were concerned. We cite these examples simply because there are still people and religious sects who would like to interpret the Bible literally; and this is not always possible, as has been shown above.

From the viewpoint of the natural sciences, the idea expressed in the second book of Genesis that woman was formed after man was is quite absurd. There are no specific male or female characteristics in the most primitive unicellular animals and in many invertebrates; as soon as animals become more complex and more differentiated the sexes become separate, as they are in all vertebrates.

Some people may say that the fact that male and female characteristics can be shown to evolve logically is something which has nothing to do with man. We cannot accept this argument, since if we compare man with other animals and organisms we find an astonishing number of likenesses. All our important functions are like those of other creatures: if one looks at the human body it becomes clear that we belong to a particular branch of the vertebrates, namely the mammals, and that we possess all the organs found in this group. Even the reproduction and fostering of offspring are the same, and it can also be shown that certain animal hormones when administered to other species produce an identical reaction to that which occurs in human beings. Everything points to our being very closely related to animals. We are dependent on the same materials for food, and we breathe the same air; obviously we are simply a part of life as a whole.

Skeletal remains are not the only or even the most vital evidence needed for an understanding of the secrets of evolution, although the evolution of the horse has been brilliantly demonstrated through the study of skeletons. Take embryology, the science which investigates living matter in its foetal stage: it is worth noting that all the basic traits of the lower species are present in the embryonic stages of all highly evolved organisms such as mammals and human beings. Life begins as a single cell, after which the foetus looks very much like a jelly-fish. It then reaches the fish stage and gill-slits appear, very similar to those of sharks. The amphibian stage follows, and the length of the tail is reduced in relation to the short and stumpy limbs.

A detailed description of this aspect of evolution is outside the scope of this book, but it must be clear by now that the theory of evolution is based on the evidence of living matter and not solely on skeletal remains. It is ridiculous to suggest that the entire theory is based on little more than a "poor heap of bones".

There are numerous questions to which science has not been able to provide an answer, and there are others for which those given appear to have been incorrect; so it is not surprising that people are now looking for other solutions and approaches to existing problems, as well as trying to find explanations of those mysteries which are still unsolved. But it will not do to treat science like the rusted-up wheels of some clockwork mechanism that needs oiling; in fact, it is man who is at fault, in that he is unable to keep pace spiritually at a time of almost unimaginable technological development. It is perhaps too late to realize that a comparable degree of intellectual development is essential if we are to avoid perishing through our own skills—which is not altogether fanciful now that we can destroy ourselves with nuclear means.

One can blame everything on science except mankind's own helplessness; only recently have people begun to realize that our spiritual development has only just begun to develop and that we still have a long way to go; and as a result we are being given some valuable—as well as some valueless—new ideas. Many of you will have read the works of Von Daniken, Charroux, Pauwels, Bergier and Kolosimo, all of whom are doing good work in publishing new ideas about man's evolution: but whether the theory that our development was influenced by extra-terrestrial agencies will prove to be true or not is something we would like to leave open for the time being. But to quote the Bible as evidence to prove the theory is going too far. As we saw at the beginning of this chapter, the Bible gives us various Creation stories: they are not to be taken as biological, scientific or astronomical statements but as *the basis for a religious vision of the world and reality*.

As a result the remarkable biblical interpretations put forward by these writers must be viewed in an altogether different light. Flying objects, fire, lightning, storms and other natural phenomena are eagerly cited by these people as evidence of the existence of rockets, "sky-chariots", amphibious helicopters and so forth. We believe that some of the scientific conclusions drawn from a reading of the Bible are absurd: for example, the Ark of the Covenant is said to have been electrically charged because anyone who touched it when it threatened to capsize fell dead as if struck by lightning. It is also claimed that a current of several hundred volts was discharged when the commandments handed down by Moses were reconstructed: a claim that is supported by talk of a condenser with gold plates, magnets, loudspeakers, a transmitter and the sparks which were said to have been emitted, although it is obvious that how all this was supposed to work is not described in any detail.

Many extraordinary stories have been told about the Ark of the Covenant. According to Silvio Gesell, a German economist,

Moses used the Ark as a laboratory for the production of gun-powder when he was at the court of the pharaoh Rameses, in which he was assisted by Jethro, his father-in-law, who as a priest had access to secret sciences. The formula is supposed to have been given in Exodus 30:34–8. Similarly, the burning bush is claimed to be the work of Moses and his father-in-law, and their "secret and magical powers" drove on the Egyptian war-chariots, made the rock split open when Moses touched it, and so on.

It is a bad point of departure to maintain that "everything is possible until the opposite is proved", since to do so is to recognize an enormous number of possibilities of which one only will be correct in the long run! If we decide against taking the Bible literally we then have to find a new explanation of creation and evolution, and this is a problem we can approach philosophically by examining various possibilities in order to reach a solution acceptable at least to modern philosophers.

The philosophical "model" for creation and evolution is merely *one* possibility; another and more concrete possibility is suggested by the efforts of science to find an explanation, particularly in the fields of biochemistry and microbiology.

An example is the recent synthesis of DNA and RNA, which apparently suggests that mankind will be able in future—perhaps in the very near future—to manufacture artificially the basic essentials of life. A centuries-old dream (or nightmare?) will then become reality: without the aid of RNA or DNA we will be able to rearrange a simple and small quantity of inorganic material in such a way that it becomes organic, as a result of which we will be able to create living organisms at a later stage.

Impossible? Insane? No, just a twentieth-century nightmare in which mankind produces new life on our planet; and the indications that such things are possible are unavoidable.

In 1953, when he was still studying at Chicago University, Doctor Stanley Miller began experiments which have since become famous. Basing his work on the theories of the Russian thinker Oparin and the American Nobel prizewinner, Professor

88

Urey, he isolated certain substances of a kind which must have been present in the primeval atmosphere when the world arose. The experiments took place under absolutely sterile conditions, and to simulate the original atmosphere as much as possible he put an electrical discharge through his mixture of ammonia, methane and hydrogen, thus ensuring that he reproduced the stormy conditions which must have characterized the weather at that time. It was hoped to achieve a kind of simultaneous chain-reaction at the same time, similar to that which must have occurred during the earliest period of earth's history; and after a week organic substances did indeed appear to be present, together with basic particles of protein molecules.

Other researchers continued his experiments with modified techniques, the substances used being changed to nitrogen, formaldehyde and carbon dioxide, while laser beams or ultrasonic waves replaced the electrical charges. The results were the same. Countless amino-acids and even a form of primitive nucleic acid were created, as a result of which one is justified in saying that we are well on the way to synthesizing life in laboratory conditions.

All of us wonder at times about the origin of life. Some find adequate explanation in the Bible, while others refuse to take the Bible literally any more but still believe in a kind of "supreme being", a creative, living and guiding power that exists somewhere in the universe. Everyone looks for some explanation or other—and nearly everyone is beset by all sorts of frustrations in his search.

As an example of this, anyone brought up in a severely religious way will be handicapped in a rather similar way to a scientist or academic with a highly specialized training. One's ideas are influenced in no small measure by one's background: and in this hunt for the truth knowledge itself may help us, but it is not the real object of the search. We cannot pretend that we have solved or even begun to solve the riddles of creation and of evolution!

But what we *can* do is to look for possible explanations and go as far back as we can in asking ourselves questions about all the phenomena with which we come in contact on this earth. If it is likely that we shall one day be able to manufacture life, we may well have to move towards a "regenerative" view of the universe, according to which new entities in space are developing constantly from gaseous clouds according to definite laws: and some of these new bodies or planets may contain the potential for developing intelligent life. What controls or causes the creation and regeneration of the universe? Science, the Bible and philosophy can all help us to understand the creation and evolution of our own world; but can they help to explain the universe? We can look for possible explanations, but they must have some foundations to them!

Just as the discovery of fossils helps us to prove the truth of evolution so, too, do other sciences and disciplines. In recent years people have reproached science for all sorts of reasons—and for trying to explain too much, among other things—yet science involves the search for truth, and it is impossible to avoid making mistakes in the process.

The already-mentioned image of science as compared to a rusted clockwork mechanism should be replaced by one of a small boy trying to build a model with his Meccano set but only succeeding after dismantling it and starting again from scratch time and again. By this we mean that one need not reject everything proposed by science simply because one disagrees with particular conclusions: science can be used, as we have seen, in helping one to make up one's mind about, and understand discoveries which have been made.

Here we must say that we certainly don't slavishly comply with all the demands made by science; instead we make use of those aspects which are acceptable to us, namely those which have had their trimmings removed. We definitely do not agree with everything put forward by scientists; but must we therefore ignore the validity of that scientific material which *is* useful and relevant to us?

# Chapter Seven

The Prehistory of ancient America—where did the native Americans originate?—the inspiration of Tiahuanaco—were the Chinese among the early inhabitants of America? —the baby and his dummy.

The stylistic tricks and the fanciful approach of some authors can occasionally mislead the reader, especially when something is only implied rather than stated outright. Examples of this are statements like "Tiahuanaco, the world's oldest town", and "the gods deliberated about mankind in Teotihuacan before *Homo sapiens* ever appeared". A couple of brief statements such as these can have a far-reaching influence; first of all it will be assumed that Tiahuanaco, which lies on the western side of Titicaca Lake in Bolivia, is the oldest city in the world, and secondly that the "gods" took counsel about humanity before *Homo sapiens* arose.

A different theory will be advanced in this book, but in order to clarify matters in general we shall begin by examining the way America was first peopled, and then discuss the early American cultures.

Really primitive types of human being such as Java or Peking man have never been found in the New World, nor indeed any anthropoid apes from which man might have developed. All past and present-day New World apes belong to the so-called "broad-nosed" groups which, unlike the Old World small-nosed apes, are fairly closely related in many respects to the primitive half-apes.

Anthropologists are agreed that it was only during the last Würm Ice Age—there were four Ice Ages, clearly separate from each other—that *Homo sapiens* crossed the Bering Strait from Asia to America. This was probably not very difficult, since the water-level during the Ice Age was very low, so they could have reached the Alaskan land-bridge which existed. They probably followed cold-climate animals which were themselves following the retreating ice and it is quite likely that these people reached America without realizing at the time that it was a different continent. At the close of the Ice Age this migration ceased; the water-level rose again, making it impossible for men or beasts to cross.

All these immigrants were of the proto-mongoloid race, and as such were related to the peoples of North-East Asia. In all probability these racial traits were diluted in time as they mixed with different peoples; and American Indians show considerable variations of type among themselves. It is quite clear that the further American Indians live from the Bering Strait (and therefore the earlier their ancestors are likely to have left Asia), the fewer typical mongoloid features they have—features which have been retained most strongly by the Eskimoes, who crossed over last of all.

It is also thought likely that all the immigrants looked much alike at first but that hereditary differences arose as a result of inter-marriage or isolation, or perhaps because of very considerable climatic variations between the places in which they settled.

The earliest traces of human habitation in America are thought to be about 12,000 years old; this has been ascertained by the use of the Carbon 14 method on the bones, charcoal, stone implements and animal remains that have been found. We often hear stories that America was populated much earlier than this, but attempts to prove that man originated in America have always failed. Ameghino was an important Argentinian advocate of these theories. Basing his work on the intelligence-level of the Capuchin ape, aboriginal legends and Maya art, he also found a number of fossil bones in the loess of the Argentinian pampas which he considered provided crucial and decisive support for his case. Relying on these finds, he elaborated whole families of apes which he provided with a plentiful supply of interesting Latin names; he also attempted to reconstruct various primitive types of human beings, for which purpose he used some incomplete and disfigured skulls, but after his work had initially attracted the attention of anthropologists it faded away without trace.

Some years ago, according to newspaper accounts, Neanderthal skulls were found in Chile, but it is now clear that all these discoveries of early remains were either the fruits of the imagination or outright deception.

Similarly the claims made for crude hand-axes which were said to have been found in America, together with various implements of a primitive type never found in the Old World, were proved to be groundless.

However, there is some justification for the claim that man reached America 20,000 or even 40,000 years ago, since no decorated arrow or spearheads have been found among the tools of these new inhabitants which are similar to those used in Siberia at the same time; in other words, the techniques used in their manufacture had developed in Siberia only *after* America had been populated and the journey via the Bering Strait was no longer possible.

Some years ago a splendid quantity of tools made of obsidian (vitreous lava) was unearthed at El Inga, high up in the Andes Mountains near Quito. These tools not only connect the various manufacturing techniques of North and South America, but many of them also show similarities in numerous respects to those found in France belonging to the Late Palaeolithic age. We can therefore assume that a comparable culture must have existed in Asia as well, so that one might expect stone tools to be found in China or Asiatic Russia, from whence came the direct antecedents of the earliest New World cultures. Once this can be shown the case—and there are enough Carbon 14 figures to support it—it will be possible to give a more precise date to the arrival of man in America.

It is often held that Red Indian languages are related to some Asiatic tongues, but this has yet to be demonstrated to be the case. The American Indian languages are very numerous, comprising more than a hundred families, and frequently the

93

differences even between neighbouring tribes are so pronounced that one might almost say that they bear about as much resemblance to each other as Dutch does to Chinese. On the one hand this suggests a lengthy and isolated development, on the other that the people who crossed from Asia to America must have had different languages *before* they crossed the Bering Strait.

For thousands of years the newly arrived Indians lived as nomadic hunters; their stone spearheads have often been found, together with the skeletons of now-extinct animals. Even in the extreme south very old human settlements have been discovered.

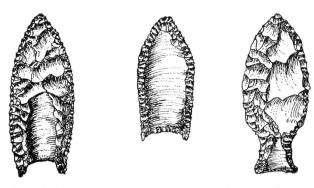

Fig. 17. Typical stone artefacts made by the first inhabitants of America. From left to right: Clovis, Folsom and Fell's Cave spearheads.

A special form of stone spearhead belonging to the early American Indians is seen in the so-called Clovis and Folsom tips (fig. 17). They are of a type entirely unknown outside America, and may thus be seen as America's oldest "patent"! But the first stages of man's existence in America were quite different from the Middle East and Europe, the basic distinction being that in the Old World domestic animals were kept first, whereas in Mexico and South America men concentrated on the cultivation and propagation of plants. The most important of these was maize, and excavations of a number of dry cavities in Mexico have proved that from about 7000 years ago corn-cobs improved continuously in size and quality as a result of better methods of farming. As a result, the harvest was greatly increased, while the wild types of maize eventually died out.

Similarly, their stone implements improved in quality, and at about the same time earthenware pestles were manufactured for the production of maize-flour; yet the people who made these utensils in Mexico still lived mainly in caves, holes and shelters behind overhanging ledges of rock. It was not until between 5000 and 3000 years ago that they began to construct primitive huts, shortly after which we find them producing clay figurines, usually representing women. These were manufactured in large numbers and in a variety of styles, but it is not easy to assess their purpose and exact age accurately. However, their relative ages can be ascertained by comparing styles.

Apart from these clay images, these primitive village communities produced little else in the way of art or religion. Religious centres like Tiahuanaco appeared only after it was realized that farming and the hybridization of maize was entirely dependent upon the sun and rain: priests then carried out impressive rites in the belief that such things could beneficially influence the rainfall and exorcize "evil spirits".

According to some popular scientific works on the subject, Tiahuanaco is of such great antiquity that the date of its origin cannot be assessed. This seems unlikely, even though the earliest cultures in America certainly have not yet been investigated sufficiently. The fact of the matter is that more has been written about the ruins of Tiahuanaco—and also more nonsense—than about any other city in the world. Even the research worker, Poznansky, who has contributed so much to conservation and exploration, is not free from the charge of having aired a number of highly speculative theories.

When the Spaniards brought their "culture" to South America they were struck by the fact that everywhere they looked they saw the ruins of vast temples, cities and fortifications, the origins of which were a complete mystery even to the civilized Incas. These widespread ruins proved that Peru, for example, already had a long history; yet all knowledge of this early civilization had been lost in the course of time. The only form of writing possessed by the Incas consisted of little more than a bundle of knotted ropes known as the "quipú": it has quite reasonably been assumed that they tried to develop a more sophisticated form of writing, but no proof of this has yet been found.

So in spite of their high level of culture and organizational ability the Incas were unable to record events; nothing of their early history was recorded, with the result that nearly all their legends and historical accounts were forgotten. Archaeologists once believed that the remains of Tiahuanaco are about 3000 years old, but today it is assumed that its large and famous buildings were built several centuries after the beginning of our era. According to the legend, Tiahuanaco was built in a single day, but its five different periods of construction clearly contradict such a claim! Furthermore, the city was devastated and rebuilt several times, Tiahuanaco was no ordinary city, but was a great religious centre. The early history of America is rich in such places, and Tiahuanaco is typical of them.

Around A.D. 600 a new god came into being here on this cold plateau almost 4000 metres about sea-level. The site is above the tree-line and is surrounded by a bare, desolate landscape. The stark, unnatural representation of this god on the Sun-gate depicts a short, thick-set body with a large head on top of which are decorations representing the rays of the sun as well as carvings of pumas. The god's face is large compared with the rest of its body, and tears are streaming out of its staring eyes. Both the puma heads and the tears are special features of this god, and in their formal style as seen at Tiahuanaco are to be found widely in Bolivia and Chile.

Quite apart from the question of why there should be a religious centre high up on a barren, chilly plateau, there is the problem of where this whole civilization and especially its artistic-religious expression originated. When one looks at its architectural achievements, particularly the great temple ruins, one is disturbed in the same way as one is when one contemplates, let us say, the Egyptian pyramids. Where did they obtain their expertise? Here again there is nothing to suggest that a

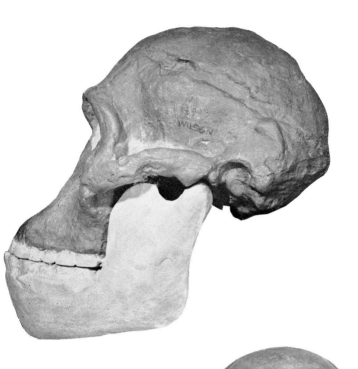

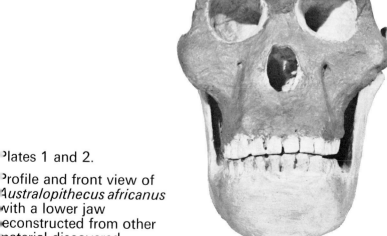

Plates 1 and 2.

Profile and front view of
*Australopithecus africanus*
with a lower jaw
reconstructed from other
material discovered.

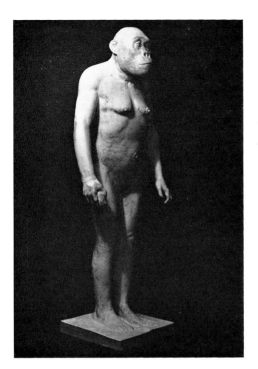

Plate 3.

A reconstruction based on the remains of a female skeleton of *Australopithecus* (*Plesianthropus*). Also known as "Mrs Ples".

Plate 4.

*Zinjanthropus* must have looked roughly like this.

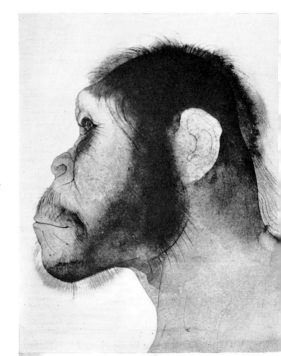

Plate 5. The famous skull-dome of *Pithecanthropus erectus Dubois*. This skull is preserved in Leiden, Holland, and is as carefully guarded as the Crown Jewels. A little-known fact about it, but a piquant one, is that its dark-brown colour, so often wrongly thought to be due to great age, in fact resulted from Dubois having originally boiled it in glue to preserve it; this came to light a few years ago when a flake of stone had been removed from the inside of the skull, which was much lighter where the stone had been.

Plate 6. A reconstruction of Java man.

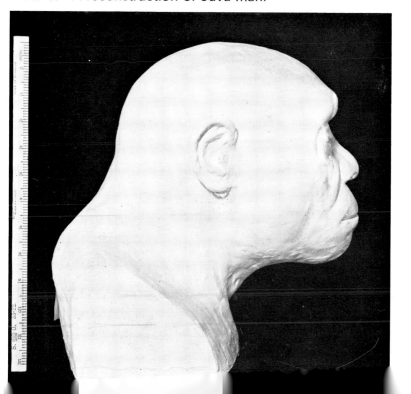

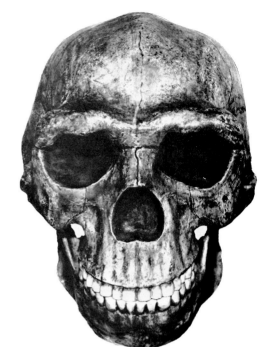

Plate 7.

Reconstructed skull of Peking man (*Sinanthropus pekinensis*).

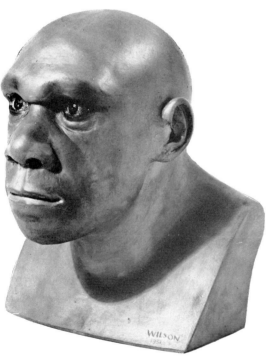

Plate 8.   Reconstruction of a West European Neanderthal. Traits: prominent eyebrow ridge, low forehead and receding chin.

Plate 9. Skull of "Swanscombe man", the oldest example of *Homo sapiens* found so far.

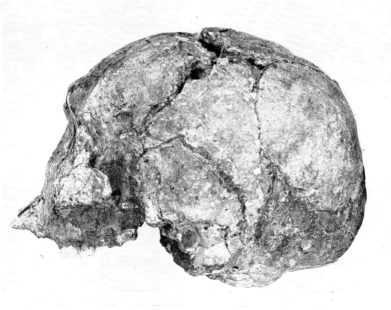

Plate 10. The Wadjak skull.

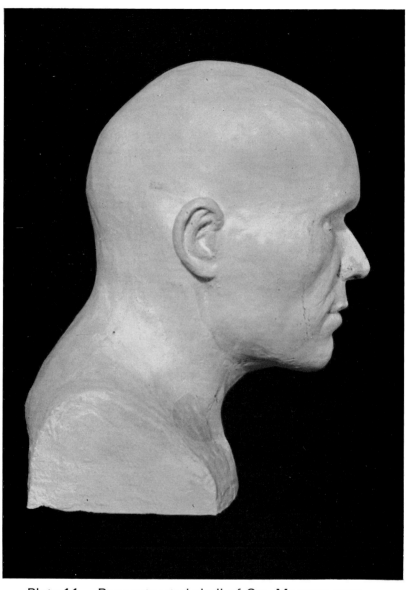

Plate 11. Reconstructed skull of Cro-Magnon man, clearly diverging from that of Neanderthal.

Plate 12.

A milestone from the reign of Melishipak the Second. Left to right: the very familiar symbols of Venus, Moon and Sun.

Plate 13.

King Scorpion's clubhead.

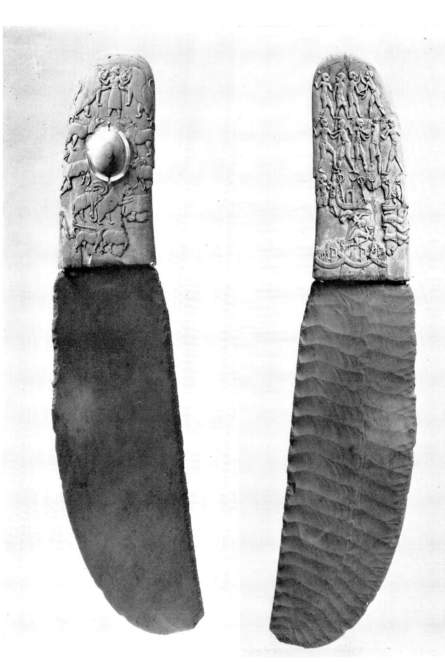

Plates 14 and 15. One side of the Gebel el Arak knife shows the Mesopotamian hero conquering two lions. On the other there are two lines of ships.

gradual development took place. The bricklaying we see in the buildings in Tiahuanaco is among the most solid and skilful in the Andes; and it is remarkable that large blocks of stone of different sizes should have been held in place by copper clamps. Despite the fact that for centuries the city was thoroughly looted for building materials, its ruins are still imposing, and it needs little imagination to visualize how it must once have looked.

There was some kind of a fortress or shelter which must have been important because of the presence of the temples, and we can still see the remains of houses which were mainly inhabited by priests. The city's stone water-supply system had its source of supply high up in the Andes at the point where the snow began to melt; canals were dug to provide a subterranean supply, and there was some kind of reservoir underneath the largest of the stepped pyramids, with an overflow canal leading to the outside.

That the cultural activities of Tiahuanaco were not confined to the construction of huge temples can be seen from its spendidly coloured tapestries and decorated pottery. Bronze was discovered, silver was mixed with copper and gold, and even solder was used: and gold and silver filigree work was also known to them. There were numerous pictures of animals, especially those of a feline nature, together with condors and snakes.

Because the city was built on a site which was too cold and high to produce any harvest worth speaking of it never attracted an extensive population, but remained a "sacred and secret" religious centre inhabited almost solely by the ruling priests.

At this point it is worth mentioning that as soon as evidence is produced of an early civilization anywhere in the world, a number of books appear which emphasize the mysterious qualities of its site. So Tiahuanaco has been widely put forward in support of the theory that "proofs" have been discovered that at some stage in human evolution an "extra-terrestrial civilization" had a hand in our affairs.

Leaving aside this particular question, it seems that Tiahuanaco does have something special about it. Figure 18 shows a diagram known in countless other places as well as in Tiahuanaco; there is nothing strange about it to anyone who has studied ancient American civilization, which possesses many examples of this particular motif. But in fact it has nothing to do with ancient America! This splendidly stylized "devil-mask", representing two dragons turned towards each other, actually occurs on a three-legged kettle from the Chinese Shang Period!

Fig. 18.

Other affinities between ancient China and America can be found in the feline godheads, lion-shaped thrones and other symbolic figures, including toys. What is the meaning of these similarities? Do they indicate that somewhere in the distant past there must have been contact between the Chinese of the Shang Period and people in ancient America? Or perhaps that they had something in common as the descendants of the surviving Ancients?

It is not impossible! From a chronological point of view in particular, it is quite certain that the early American cultures cannot be ascribed to any actions of those Ancients we have already mentioned: yet we must seriously consider the suggestion that when they first developed there was some contact with the Ancients, as a result of which they were able to flourish in the way they did. In other words, their sudden cultural development was due to the Ancients, or rather to their descendants.

If we consider things logically, we cannot assume that Columbus was the first person from the Old World to discover the New! More and more evidence is being put forward to convince us that there were links between the Old and the New Worlds *much* earlier than Columbus! This view is still fiercely contested —we almost said "naturally"—but towards the end of the book we shall prove convincingly that Columbus did not discover America!

Fig. 19.   The god-head of the Tiahuancao Sun-gate.

Those who do not doubt the "myth of Tiahuanaco" mention a "primitive mother" with only four fingers; they also draw attention to the fact that the sun-god pictures on the Tiahuanaco sun-gate also has only four fingers on each hand (fig. 19). But are they aware that on other monuments the same god in fact shows all five fingers?

In the Bible (1 Chronicles 20:6 and Samuel 21:20) mention is made of a man of "great height" with "six fingers and toes". But it is a fact—albeit a rare one—that there are people with a different number of fingers and toes from the normal. This

Fig. 20.

deviation, known as polydactylism, frequently occurs among cats, which sometimes have six or even seven toes without the slightest disadvantage to themselves.

It is going a little too far to make assertions about the anatomy of the hand that are based on legends, statues of gods and primitive rock drawings. All over the world one can find pictures of people carrying things without showing any of their fingers at all; yet nobody would claim that in fact they had four or six fingers simply because they happened to be concealed!

Again it is claimed that the sun-god of Tiahuanaco is surrounded by secret symbols in the figures accompanying him: these are said to represent a "space-diver", an unknown machine, a jet-engine, a solar battery, a retro-rocket, a space vehicle and finally a space-ship (fig. 20).

If we were to claim that we could clearly see in the head a baby in pyjamas howling for his dummy, nobody could prove that this was not the case. We come back to the question of how one should interpret pictures of this kind. Are we to use a kind of Rorschach test, in which one can see anything one likes in the separate parts of the picture; or should one look at the thing as

100

a whole, in which case independent and highly subjective verdicts are more difficult to make convincingly?

In this chapter we have put forward our opinions and our theories without wanting to attack either conventional science or the protagonists of different ideas. By putting forward new theories we run the risk of being associated with a particular group of people or set of ideas, and in order to prevent this happening to some extent, we would like to state quite categorically that our opinions have developed principally from our own interpretations of discoveries that have been made, and that we have relied on logical reasoning to support our arguments.

In arriving at a decision we were neither entirely dependent on science nor tied to other people's theories. We appreciate that our own theories are not necessarily the correct ones and we would like other and different theorists to receive all the credit that is due to them. Let all of us have our own beliefs: time will show who is right!

# Chapter Eight

The enigmatic "people's migration" of the Mayas—the Maya calendar and arithmetic—jade, the stone of the gods? —Palenque still keeps us busy.

Anyone familiar with the history of the ancient American civilizations will have come across the Mayas in his studies. He will also have read that there was a Maya migration of population round about A.D. 600 which involved the complete abandonment of their towns and temples in order to found a new kingdom in the north.

Recent researchers have shown that this story must be modified in certain important respects. In the first place, the Mayas gave up their flourishing temple cities about A.D. 890 to 900 rather than at the date given above. We can deduce this from the fact that after these dates no more calendar inscriptions can be found on columns—indeed no columns were erected later than this period.

Similarly it has proved that to talk of a population migration is too all-embracing, since there was no question of a wholesale departure: they simply turned their backs on their old religious centres.

The reason for this is not yet entirely clear: the end of the classical Maya period is just as problematic as its beginning. It is unlikely that war played a part in the story, and no indications have come to light of any climatic variation or epidemic outbreaks. Some people argued that the primitive farming methods of the times might have so exhausted the soil in the long run that starvation resulted: yet the sites are so fertile that even with the crudest methods it must have remained possible to obtain good harvests from them. How is it that a land that was able to feed its population so well for many centuries should suddenly become infertile—in a space of two years at the most? The following explanation may be the correct one!

A striking fact which is usually overlooked is revealed in the columns used by the Mayas for Ancient Kingdom inscriptions, which have subsequently been deliberately damaged. Of particular interest are the faces on these columns, since in some cases they are the only parts to have been damaged, which might well indicate that there was a popular uprising against the prevailing religious rulers.

Further evidence in support of this theory is the fact that there is no indication that the highly developed calendar system was still in use in the post-classical period; and the columns containing data about the "long" addition method are entirely absent. It seems extremely likely that the elaborate system of calculations disappeared after this rebellion, together with the priests who were responsible for carrying it out.

In keeping with our other chapters about ancient cultures, we shall examine these calendars and calculations—which in this case are almost unbelievable.

Unlike Mayan writing, which is as yet still undeciphered—though every year one hears of someone who claims to have done so—the numeration system in its relation to the calendar is understood, as is its significance for divinities and planetary events. One of the earliest known actual events in Mayan culture dates back to about 31 B.C.; some calculations like those of Quiriga go back as far as 400 million years ago, but these figures appear to have been worked out by the priests either as a joke or as an example of their power.

A numeration system was developed by the Mayas and other Central American civilizations which was based on units of twenty, most likely from the total number of fingers and toes, as opposed to that employing the ten fingers only, which eventually led to the decimal system. Other very special features were the use of positional notation and the employment of a sign for zero. Both may have been discovered independently by the Mayas, whose culture arose long before the start of the Christian era: they were first used in India in the fourth century of our era, but it was only thanks to the Arabs that they reached Europe in later medieval times.

It also seems strange that Mayan mathematical methods were better and more efficient than those of the Greeks and Romans, even in the construction of the symbols. The Mayas had two

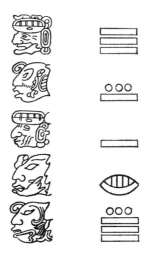

Fig. 21. Both these columns of symbols represent the number 2,466,018. The analysis of how this total is arrived at is shown below.

$$
\begin{array}{rcl}
15 \times 160{,}000 &=& 2{,}400{,}000 \\
8 \times 8000 &=& 64{,}000 \\
5 \times 400 &=& 2000 \\
0 \times 20 &=& 0 \\
18 \times 1 &=& 18\ + \\
\hline
& & 2{,}466{,}018
\end{array}
$$

different methods of stating in writing any figure from 1 to 19 and 0. They made use of a system of dots and lines which was simple and easy to understand—one might compare it with our Roman signs—as well as a kind of hieroglyphic (fig. 21).

The simplest system, and it was a miracle of simplicity, was the application of dots and lines (1 dot = 1, 1 line = 5) which may have developed from the habit of placing small stones and

104

sticks on the ground during calculations. It may be that an empty snail-shell was adopted to represent zero, as would seem to be suggested by the variations known to have been used for the purpose.

The dot-line system was the standard one for the Mayas; it consists of elements which represent fixed values, as is the case with the Roman ciphers. But the Mayan system is superior in that they used only two signs for any figure from 1 to 19: in other words, 3 lines = 15 and 4 dots = 4, which together come to 19, whereas the Romans had to use three elements for the same idea, which then had to be added and subtracted (IV, IX, XIV, XIX). Is it not strange, though, that a civilization which began much later than that of the Old World was apparently able to develop—or should we say inherit—such a system?

The other method employed hieroglyphics portraying the stylized heads of gods: variations are found for each of these, but they can easily be identified by certain traits. There are thirteen different gods for the figures 1 to 13 while for numbers from 14 to 19 the same gods are used as those for 4 to 9, with the sole difference that the lower jaw is white or pale; a hand is held underneath it and a head represents zero. These variations are much like our own Arabic numerals in which there are separate signs for all the numerals from 1 to 9, as well as zero, except that among the Mayas there were separate signs all the way from 1 to 19, including zero.

In order to show place-values the Mayas put the units, the twenties, the four-hundreds, and so on, above each other, rather than behind each other as we do. In this way they obtained a column of figures which had to be read from the bottom upwards: this was a system which could express large numbers with the use of few symbols, and to make this clearer we append an example (see fig. 21).

It used to be claimed in geography books used in secondary schools that China is the only place in which jade is to be found; yet a good many writers have pointed out over the years that, oddly enough, jade was the most precious stone among all the Central American peoples, and that if it could be found only in China there must have been some sort of contact between America and the Chinese of the Shang dynasty. Although some modern encyclopaedias still state that China is the sole producer of jade, it is in fact also found in Mazanal, in the Montague valley in Guatemala. The Central American jade is chemically almost the same as the Chinese, except that it is perhaps a little less translucent and rather more speckled. Its colour depends on the chrome content and varies from dark green to bluish-green.

To work this particularly hard and tough mineral points to a high level of technical skill, particularly in view of the fact that these peoples had no metal tools for the purpose.

It is striking that jade occurs much less frequently in the New Kingdom of the Mayas, and that their manufactured articles are appreciably smaller. It is possible that the greater part of the jade-working industry and techniques disappeared along with the priests when the people rebelled against their rulers.

The paved streets of the Mayas were again supposed to have been remarkable according to some authorities, if only because they were built rather higher than is normal. However they did not use the wheel for transport—though they certainly used it for toys, and so forth—which can almost certainly be explained by the lack of draught animals.

It would be a mistake to assume from the fact that they built roads that an extensive network existed; in fact, to take one example, the city of Tikal was not linked by a road to nearby Uaxactún.

The snake is often portrayed in ancient American art, and some writers have written almost lyrically about serpents crawling through the dust and over the steaming soil since time immemorial; yet at one time snakes did in fact have limbs, remnants of which can still be seen in the anaconda, boa constrictor and python. These vestigial limbs are at the back and can be moved, though they are definitely not used for propulsion.

To Christians the snake may well seem to be the very image of evil, but the Mayas felt no such repugnance about reptiles—indeed their most important divinity was the feathered snake

Kukulkan! (Feathers symbolized the wind, and the snake the soil.)

A good deal has been written about why the Mayas did not settle near natural sources of water but instead built reservoirs in and around Tikal. Once their trade had been investigated it was learnt that from the sixth century B.C. the Mayas traded in obsidian and flint. These were found in large quantities near Tikal, which would explain why no early settlements have yet been found on the banks of the Petén Itza lake.

It is not true to say that the Mayas used no floral motifs of any kind, since the water-lily among others is not uncommon in the late and post-classical periods. Not long ago some murals were discovered in Bonampak (Chiapas) which were richly decorated with gods and water-lilies: they were somewhat stylistically reproduced, which may explain why some writers and even "experts" maintain that the Mayas had no floral art.

It would be indefensible to round off this discussion of early Mayan art and culture without mentioning the so-called tombstone of Palenque, about which Von Daniken and others have made claims which we do not intend to repudiate: once again we leave the verdict to the reader.

It was not until 1952 that the Mexican archaeologist Alberto Ruz discovered a corridor under the Temple of Inscriptions, as it is called, with two narrow steps at one end leading to a room twenty-one metres (!) deep. Having exposed the buried doorway and gone down the steps—what an experience that must have been!—he entered a vaulted chamber, in the middle of which he saw in the dim light an enormous plate made from stone, which proved to be the lid of a sarcophagus. After bringing down the required equipment the lid was carefully jacked up and the bones of a chief were brought to light. A splendid mosaic mask covered the face, and around the corpse lay roughly eight hundred beads and various jade objects. The quantity and quality of this Maya treasure has never been equalled! From the room ornaments it appeared that this chief must have been buried about A.D. 690.

Some new theories have been forwarded based on the now-familiar ornament on the lid of the sarcophagus; Von Daniken and others have suggested that it represents a space traveller. It is not difficult to refute this argument.

The lid must not be looked at horizontally but vertically, from the foot of the sarcophagus. The figure on the so-called "rocket" is then lying on its back, and in this position it seems somewhat less like a "rocket" with its "pilot"; and it is portrayed without any protective clothing outside rather than inside the "rocket". It does not require too much imagination to see technical equipment in the surrounding signs, flourishes and symbols.

Despite our ambivalent feelings about the methods of science, it is worth quoting the scientific report on this ornament by way of contrast.

> "The central motif represents a religious symbol akin to our Tree of Life. A mythical bird is sitting on the top of the Maya tree whilst the branches are in the form of grotesque celestial snakes. There is a double-headed snake twisted around some of the lateral branches and the heads of gods are close to its jaws. The tree itself rises up from behind the figure of a person who is sitting in a very uncomfortable position on the Mayas' earth monster."

The Maya posture mentioned here should be explained as the "weaving-position", which is achieved by leaning slightly backwards, a movement which makes the loom more taut. In similar drawings one sometimes finds a maize plant instead of a human figure. Are these plants really piloting space vehicles? Even in Europe one can find similar diagrams in, for instance, the Maya Codex at Dresden.

The figure depicted on the lid has the deformed skull typical of the Mayas; on the edge there are signs which stand for various celestial phenomena like the moon, sun and Venus, though they have no connection with the symbols on the Tiahuanaco sungate. Incidentally, an exact replica of the lid has now been made, and can be admired in the National Anthropological Museum in Mexico City.

Almost all books about early American civilizations—and not

just the popular science publications—mention the great "candlestick symbol" of the Gulf of Pisco. It has been suggested that it may be either a seismograph or some sort of guide for space vehicles flying overhead, but it seems more likely that it was a beacon for fishermen coming into port. If it were a seismograph it would have to reproduce sound waves in the Earth's crust! And how could this be done? The idea that it was a beacon for space craft is more acceptable, except for the fact that the drawing was made on a vertical rock-wall rather than on the open roof above, where it might have been more easily seen. Was it then a beacon for shipping as we believe?

To sum up, the ancient civilizations of America were both impressive and highly developed. There appears to have been a long and slow transition from the Stone Age to the time when the great cultures began to flourish: once again we must ask *how* these civilizations came into being, bearing in mind their similarities with ancient China as well as the legendary accounts of the arrival of "fair-haired men with blue eyes", the gods from the Old World. It is becoming ever clearer that *long* before the time of Columbus the Chinese or another great seafaring race enjoyed the world's greatest experience—the discovery of America!

# Chapter Nine

Metalworking techniques?—the platinum mystery—stainless steel in ancient times?—the oldest phonetic script in the world?

Our discussions of ancient civilizations would be incomplete if we did not say something about metalworking and writing. We have dealt with these skills as practised among less well-known cultures since anyone can without too much difficulty turn to reference books containing large numbers of articles about the best-known and most important civilizations; we will now discuss developments in the ancient American cultures which had their own peculiarities regarding metalworking methods, for instance, and we will examine the "rust-proof" iron columns of Delhi and elsewhere. As far as the art of writing is concerned, we have chosen one that is not commonly referred to, namely the Glozel discoveries in France, which are still a puzzle to archaeologists.

It is well-known that large quantities of gold were used in metalwork, especially in Central and South American cultural regions; what is less publicized is the fact that this metal was not only employed in the manufacture of ornaments but also for useful articles like fish-hooks, needles and even nails. These small objects of daily use are evidence of the amazing skill of the craftsmen who made them.

But it was not only gold that glittered: in Antioquia, northern Columbia, objects have been unearthed made of an alloy consisting of 50% copper, 33% gold and 12% silver. This was called "tumbago" or "tumbaga"; and this explains why it has often been claimed that this gold had only half the normal weight because of a "mysterious weight-displacement", since the specific gravity of copper is less than half that of gold.

La Tolita in Ecuador has a different form of gold which often contains platinum. Platinum has become a very precious metal owing to present-day industrial requirements, but in the time of the Incas it was by no means so highly valued: it was looked upon mainly as a substitute for silver. Nevertheless investigators were struck by the occurrence of this alloy of platinum and gold.

Gold, silver and copper are relatively easy to smelt since they fuse at around 1000° C.; but platinum has a melting-point of almost 1800° C. It was first assumed that platinum could only be made into an alloy with gold by smelting. Naturally enough these discoveries attracted the attention of the specialized scientific publications as well as of popular works on the subject; and it turned out that the "Red Indians" could use platinum in almost anything they wished to. The La Tolita site revealed not only jewels and nose-rings made of this metal but also very fine plates, one side of which was in gold and the other platinum.

How did the ancient metalworkers manage to make this alloy at a time when the modern smelting-oven did not exist? How could they reach such extremely high temperatures?

At first it seemed impossible to find out in detail about pre-Columbian metalworking techniques as far as gold and platinum were concerned; however, further research at La Tolita revealed that not one of all the thousands of objects found had actually been cast. They were all made of thin wire or foil hammered together by smiths; there was no evidence of solder having been used, and it became evident that the materials had been hammered together cold to give them extra strength. The same process had been used for other objects made of bronze, gold or copper.

Gradually, then, the enigma was resolved. It was learnt next that pure silver could not apparently be found, and that the silver content so often found in the gold must have been already present in it.

What made the La Tolita discoveries so important was the presence of a large number of articles which exemplified almost all the different stages of metalworking, and in this way it was possible to trace the various processes through from the start.

A quantity of flat discs were discovered with crystals on the surface resulting from the fluidity of the metal. It was shown that charcoal had been used in the smelting, with extra oxygen being added by means of a blow-pipe—a technique that is known elsewhere in South America—and the imprints of the charcoal could be seen clearly underneath the discs. A large quantity of gold was used in the form of plates, square blocks and bars: three other specimens were found which showed that gold had also been used in the production of wire. The wire had a maximum thickness of 2 mm. and a minimum of 0·1 mm., which was achieved by re-heating the original wires drawn from the wedges and then pulling them out.

Further research into the secrets of ancient metalworking techniques finally resolved the "platinum riddle". These investigations showed that the platinum contained about 30% gold, which itself contained a proportion of silver. By examining specimens in which the processes had either been left unfinished or had been at fault, the investigators gained an insight into a very special technique. The raw platinum grains had been mixed with some gold and then heated, during which process the whole mass became fused. This is a well-known process today: if you re-heat a metal and add to it another quantity of metal that has not yet been smelted, the former will diffuse into the latter after continuous heating. In the case of the gold and platinum the mass became clotted, and after repeated hammerings and re-heating was homogeneous enough to be used in sheets or other forms. Such sheets could later be fused with gold, for instance, so that fairly thin sheets could be finally obtained for further manufacture.

So forging was the answer, and not smelting. Put like this it looks very simple, yet a large number of expert research workers spent a long time solving the problem of how people were able to carry out platinum metalworking with primitive techniques —or are they really primitive?

We must now look at a rather less costly metal which has for a long time attracted the attention of a large number of experts and laymen alike: iron.

The belief that present-day iron is of lower quality than in ancient times has been maintained throughout the centuries. Pliny claimed that there was a large chain in the city of Zegma on the Euphrates and that Alexander the Great had made a bridge out of it to cross the river; and that while the new links had been attacked by rust the old ones had stayed completely free of it.

Another version of the same story is that of the so-called Iron Pillar of Delhi, erected by a group of engineers in the distant past "who wanted to leave to the world an immortal and visible monument. They therefore erected the rust-proof Iron Pillar of Delhi which was of a secret composition and alleged to be about 4000 years old."

Iron appeared in northern India around 1000 B.C. and about 500 years later in the south; ironworking was carried on at that time by travelling blacksmiths. The numerous iron weapons excavated from burial sites and the erection of pillars of this metal at Delhi and elsewhere all point to the fact that the techniques of ironworking gradually improved as the centuries wore on. However, it soon became clear that the columns could not be very ancient since they were constructed almost immediately after the close of the earliest phase of ironworking. Both the techniques employed and the dimensions of the columns prove that they could only have been the product of an established iron industry; which rules out the possibility of itinerant blacksmiths having made them. Most of the columns have Buddhist laws and inscriptions on them and they were separately erected, largely for decorative purposes, during the period of the first great Kingdom of India.

The most famous of all, the Delhi Pillar, is almost seven metres high and is covered with writing, as a result of which the date of its erection was estimated to be A.D. 310. Other pillars of the same type were put up around that time. On all of them are found Asoka pronouncements, which are more usually found cut into rock.

The Indians used an ore which occurred abundantly in some parts of their country and contained, on average, 72·39% red ironstone. It is clear that the pillars themselves were made by smelting together iron discs, and that they are splendid examples of what could be done even with primitive techniques. The Delhi column itself has been the subject of a good many investigations over a century, in the course of which the following explanations have been put forward to account for the total absence of rust:

—The absolute purity of the metal.
—Since a stone anvil was used the surface received a coating of silicone, which prevented rusting.
—The iron contained layers of large amounts of ash; the rust reached these layers but got no farther.
—The pillar was covered with a thin layer of cinders.

These possibilities were soon rejected. The extraordinarily low level and even the total absence of sulphur could be attributed to the purity of the charcoal used in the smelting process. A large number of investigations finally led to the conclusion that where one column was rusted and another remained free of rust, the cause was to be found in the local environment.

The composition of the pillars* was no longer seen as the chief reason for the absence of rust. Much was made of the surface condition of the pillar, which was like highly polished bronze. (An old religious custom consisted of smearing the surface with butter during certain ceremonies, and this was also taken into account!)

The answer to the problem was very different from what one might expect. For centuries after the erection of the Delhi Pillar the atmosphere remained free from pollution, and its great distance from the sea excluded any possibility of there being salt deposits from the air. The aridity of the climate was enough to ensure that the column was hardly ever subjected to rainfall. In such a hot and salt-free climate what little rust there was attacking the metal actually worked as a protective barrier against

* The Delhi Pillar consists of: 99·72% iron; 0·114% phosphorus; 0·08% carbon; 0·046% silicon; 0·032% nitrogen; plus a few traces of copper and other elements.

further rusting. The rust-free state of the columns was also attributed in part to wind-borne sand which must have polished the metal.

It is worth noting in support of this argument that in some districts of India nowadays certain types of modern steel are outstandingly useful: the actual rails on the railways appear to be in perfect condition after thirty-five years, and iron-plated wagons built in 1883 are still free of rust provided that they are employed in the same area as that of the Delhi Pillar. The same type of wagons when used in Burma or on the Bombay coast failed to remain in a respectable condition for more than a year.

We might also add that samples of metal from the Delhi Pillar began to rust after only *one* night when placed near water in a laboratory, as did the sample sent with so much publicity to England. It has recently been shown that the part of the column which is underground has suffered considerable damage from rust.

The Dhar Pillar, which is usually mentioned in conjunction with that of Delhi, was made from round iron discs hammered together. The column was originally about fifteen metres high and weighed seven tons, but it is now broken into three pieces, probably as a result of religious disturbances in the fourteenth and fifteenth centuries. The dating of the pillar is not easy as there are no inscriptions on it but from its shape it seems to belong to the Gupta period (between A.D. 320 and 480), and is therefore contemporary with that of Delhi. It contains a number of holes which were probably used to hold it by and to turn the whole thing during its construction; possibly they were also of use when transporting it, since part of the column was found with the end of an iron rod wedged into it. The material of which it is made is very pure,* but the hardness of the metal varies somewhat. A sample taken from it also soon became rusty when placed in a damp laboratory atmosphere.

Finally, mention must be made of the oldest smelting foundry in the world at Ezeon Geber on the Gulf of Aqaba. It was

* Composition of the Dhar Pillar: 99·6% iron; 0·02% carbon; 0·28% phosphorus.

cleverly built so that maximum use was made of the north-westerly winds which blow almost constantly in this area; an elaborate system of air ducts and rooms ensured that the wind's force was exploited. It was a simple enough operation to re-construct the smelting process used by studying the objects and data found there. The ores were excavated in various places near the foundry and underwent a preliminary heating before being transported to Ezeon Geber. The fires were supplied with charcoal, and the already processed copper ores were laid be-tween beds of lime in large earthenware smelting crucibles with thick walls. After this the fluid copper was poured off into moulds which were either open or closed. Excavations further revealed that this copper smelting dated from around 1100 B.C. and that the copper ore had been mined from about 2000 B.C. The building seems to have been radically altered in the time of King Solomon, when it took on the shape in which the exca-vators found it.

Metals in ancient times: are you aware of the background to the special techniques involved?

\*     \*     \*

On March 1st 1924 two French farmers, Emile Fradin and his father-in-law, Claude Ziegel, were busy ploughing a strip of land along the little Vareille river in the parish of Glozel about twenty kilometres south of Vichy, when the ploughshare suddenly jammed. When they investigated the trouble they discovered the first of a whole series of finds including earthenware urns, a female figurine (plate 16), diverse bone implements (plates 17 and 18) and other objects with drawings of animals on them. But the most striking finds were some clay tablets upon which were some signs which closely resembled a form of writing (plate 19).

After consulting with other local people, the two farmers came to the conclusion that they were Roman remains, and carried on their ploughing. It was not until more than a year later that Dr Morlet from Vichy appeared on the scene. He was the first to show real interest in the finds and to appreciate their

116

| meaning; | Feniciërs | Glozel |
|:---:|:---:|:---:|
| n | ꓬ | ꓬ |
| m | ꟽ | ꟽ |
| o | O | O |
| ℓ | L | ∠ |
| t | + | + |
| ω | Y | Y |
| ẛ | ㄹ | ㅋ |
| ᵹ | 1 | 1 |
| p | ꓭ | ⟩ |
| s | W | W |

significance. He published a pamphlet entitiled *Nouvelle Station Néolithique*—a new neolithic settlement—and on his own initiative added Emile Fradin's name to it.

The result was that a kind of archaeological civil war broke out in France, which was carried on by both lawful and unlawful methods. Many French experts doubted the authenticity of the finds and even went so far as to publicly accuse Fradin and Dr Morlet of perpetrating a fraud: among them was René Dussaud, a curator at the Louvre, and when Fradin and Morlet sued him he lost the case. Dussaud could hardly be termed an entirely impartial investigator himself, a point to which we shall return.

The Glozel discoveries were at first declared to be genuine by the famous French archaeologist, the Abbé Breuil, who then withdrew his opinion and detached himself completely from anything to do with the finds; in this way he avoided being drawn into the high-level furore which developed around Glozel. The discoveries are still the subject of much controversy among French archaeologists, and heated discussions about them are likely to continue.

Foreign researchers were also involved, including some Russians, though we do not know what their opinions were. Scandinavian archaeologists also investigated the discoveries and adopted a very positive attitude to them; and there was the Spaniard, Dr Carvallo, who after being sceptical initially, wrote about them, while a B.B.C. film team prepared an objective film based on the finds.

Are they genuine or not? After more than forty-five years an answer has yet to be given, nor has a satisfactory attempt been made to date them! The signs on the objects provide the greatest stumbling-block from the point of view of the scholars, and they have led many French archaeologists to reject them entirely: on the other hand the archaeologist Salmon Reinach adopts a diametrically opposed view and believes them to be genuine artefacts and about 4000 years old.

If we compare the Glozel signs with the ancient Phoenician alphabet we can immediately see unmistakable similarities between the two: however, the Phoenician alphabet consisted of sound values and twenty-four symbols, whereas the Glozel had about forty symbols, and we do not know if there were any vowel values. It may be that the Glozel signs were a transitional language that developed from ideograms or conceptual writing: the symbol representing a bone, for instance, is the drawing of a bone without any attached vowel value unless written in a phonetic alphabet.

It is curious that among the Glozel signs the swastika or hooked cross occurs several times, which provided a reason for keeping them hidden during the Second World War in case the Nazis made use of them to give the Aryan "Master Race" theory an aura of respectability.

Those who are sceptical about Glozel claim that the whole

thing is a careful and sophisticated piece of forgery. Fradin is supposed to have admitted during a bout of drunkenness that he manufactured the objects himself, and further research is alleged to show that this was the case. But there is no evidence of any bout of drunkenness or rash statements being made under the influence of drink. Nor do we know anything about an investigation into the matter; however we do know that so far no Carbon 14 test of the artefacts has been made, but from what we know of Fradin personally he is quite prepared for such a test!

Moreover we find it difficult to imagine him working away year after year on this enormous quantity of objects. Just think! How could Fradin have produced so many objects in the little free time he enjoys? Could he really have spent every evening labouring over clay tablets, bones, pots and other objects and preparing them as carefully as possible. One must also remember that the finds were scattered over a wide area and were mostly tangled among the roots of vegetation. To bury the articles alone would have been a protracted and exacting task, placing Fradin among the greatest forgers of all time!

Experts agree that the objects were made with a high degree of skill, which means that Fradin must have had at his command all the specialized techniques of sculpture, painting, pottery, etching and modelling; yet nobody who has met this amiable man has ever been able to imagine him to be capable of all these skills. There is also the fact that Fradin and his father-in-law did not appreciate the value of what they had found for quite some time; as Morlet wrote later, "they carried on ploughing". It might be thought that Morlet was possibly the guilty party, since he was the one who brought the discoveries into the public eye; but again this would not be justified since he did not appear on the scene until at least a year later and after almost all the articles had been found.

At this point we must return to René Dussaud, as one of those who believe it is all a fraud. Dussaud was and still is the protagonist of the theory that the Phoenicians possessed the world's oldest phonetic alphabet, and that it was the precursor of our own: yet if the Glozel script was genuine, this theory of his would have to be abandoned. Bearing this in mind, are we not justified in refusing to consider him an objective judge of the matter?

The objects themselves clearly resemble those of other ancient cultures; the figurine, for instance, being very much like "mother goddesses" of the sort met in the Cyclades and in excavations at Troy. Another trait met elsewhere is the mouthless faces on the urns—a feature suggesting eternal silence—while the drawings of animals are unmistakably akin to, among others, those of the Almeria culture. It is said that the drawings of spearheads (fig. 17) suggest that they were forged, since they do not seem adequate to the purpose; but this argument hardly carries water if one bears in mind the fact that numerous implements from much older cultures have not, at first sight, looked very effective or very suitable for what they were supposed to achieve.

But it is the Glozel "script", the signs on the objects and clay tablets, to which people take the greatest exception. They point out that similar material has never been found elsewhere, so the signs and symbols are unique. But who knows what may still lie under the soil and when it may come to light? Furthermore any independent, unique find cannot immediately be assumed to be a forgery! Other discoveries of a unique nature have been made before now, and far from proving to be hoaxes they have been recognized as genuine!

In general there is much to be said both for and against the Glozel finds, so it is disheartening that no exact and rigorous dating test has ever been undertaken; a fact attributed by both sides in the controversy to the negligible amount of carbon in the finds. However, Holland has one of the best equipped institutes for Carbon 14 research (the Institute for Biology and Archaeology, led by Professor H. T. Waterbolk at Groningen), and it is a pity that these facilities have never been used in this connection. In addition to the Carbon 14 test there is also a test by which the amount of flouride, uranium and nitrogen is assessed: admittedly this method does not give the actual age of the object, but it does clearly demonstrate the presence or absence of modern bone material. There is also a form of magnetic dating, and one of the newest developments in this field is called "thermodating". The site should also be combed with a proton-magnetometer to locate further objects, if any exist.

French researchers must of course take the lead in further work in this field, but if this is not possible perhaps foreign experts could be allowed to examine the data. After forty-five years of controversy the time has come to settle the matter once and for all, and to decide the real worth of the discoveries.

We recently received a letter from Fradin in which he expressed his readiness to accept a Carbon 14 test without any reservations. He even proposed that he would choose the objects to be tested himself, while we would announce the result! Does this not prove something? It may be that the Glozel finds are the only remaining evidence of the writing used by the Ancients!

# Chapter Ten

Preparation of mummies for resurrection?—the Russians
and twentieth-century deep-freeze mummies—space travel
in ancient Japan?

Our views on mummification in Egypt and in ancient Russia
differ once again from those held by writers concerned with
extra-terrestrial influences; but when one of these writers states
that the phenomenon of Egyptian mummification has not yet
been satisfactorily explained we must acknowledge that he is
right.

Mummification in the early civilizations provides one of the
first manifestations of a belief in the "beyond"; but we do not
know what brought this belief into being. Many elaborate
explanations have been put forward but for the most part they
have been almost valueless through a lack of scientific validity.
Not *one* of them, so far, has been completely satisfactory.

In *Was God an Astronaut?* Von Daniken asks himself how the
"pagans" acquired the idea of a physical return to life? He and
his school believe that there is a cosmic influence at work, a conclusion he has been forced to by the failure of science to provide
an adequate answer. Perhaps they might even be right after all
in an indirect way. Is this a manifestation of man's unconscious
realization that he is a part of the whole universe, arising from
it and returning once again to it?

The Egyptian mummies, together with their grave-goods
intended for use in an "afterlife", have something special about
them which appeals to our imagination; but one must not think
in terms of a "mystic happening" which has nothing to do with
reality. Nor should we take literally every mention of a "bodily
return to life", since the first question we should ask is how can
living human beings be re-created from mummies?

122

It is well-known that the Egyptians disembowelled the body and removed the brains before mummifying the corpse. The organs that had been taken out were then placed in the grave in so-called "canopic" jars. There were usually four of these, and they were often made of alabaster. It is difficult to see how resurrection could take place with these vital organs missing. We must simply assume that the Egyptians did not have the necessary skill or knowledge to undertake elaborate operations on the intestines and brains and to transplant them, when they were already in an advanced state of decay, back into the mummy, which itself was decomposing despite the special treatment it had received. In order to make this clearer we shall go a little further into the process of mummification.

In earliest Egyptian times people succeeded in preserving only the shape of the body: the Memphis mummies, for instance, are completely atrophied—they are almost black and show no individual facial features whatsoever. They are also very fragile. Later on means were found of avoiding the decomposition and shrinking of the body, to a great extent, and it is only from this period that personal characteristics of the body have been retained.

When bodies were mummified the brains were removed through the nose with a metal hook, while the bowels were extracted after a large abdominal incision. The heart was supposed to be left in its place, but since the gut removal was often crudely done the heart was frequently taken out at the same time. What remained of the body was then thoroughly washed and placed in a salt bath, often for more than a month. After this the body was dried out, a process which lasted a good seventy days. As a result of all this, a completely seasoned corpse was produced, and the abdominal cavity was then filled up with such materials as loam, sand, shavings, resin and shreds of linen, together with some highly fragrant substances. Even onions were occasionally used! The body was then wrapped in linen bandages saturated with tar-like oils.

Not so long ago it was thought that the Egyptians used secret chemicals, but later analysis showed that ritual was the predominant feature of mummification rather than the less important chemical effects of the substances employed.

Finally, we are not likely to give offence to anybody if we say we think it impossible for these mummies ever to return to normal human life.

*    *    *

The so-called Russian "deep-freeze mummies" are less well-known, but they have been discussed by, among others, Von Daniken in his book *Chariots of the Gods?* The discussions about the ancient Scythians include drawings and a photograph of the "carpet" shown later in this chapter, but as far as we know no photographs of the mummies or the graves have ever appeared in the West. There was an article about the Russian Scythian graves in the monthly magazine "*Scientific American*" which appeared in May 1965 but only *one* photograph of the so-called "Persian Carpet" was shown. Some sketches and drawings have been made but they are not entirely accurate, and this lack of both precise information and photographs from behind the Iron Curtain has led to excessive speculation. Von Daniken did not have our own exclusive photographic material at his disposal, nor did he have the details we were sent from the Hermitage Museum at Leningrad; but he does have some observations to make about such finds as the Russian Rodenko (or Rudenko) mummy, which was discovered eighty kilometres from the Outer Mongolian frontier at the tomb of Kurgan V of Pazarik.

This grave consists of a stone hillock, lined with timber inside. All the burial chambers are filled with "permanent ice" so that the contents were preserved in a state of deep-freeze. One of them contained the embalmed bodies of a man and a woman, both of which had been prepared in the same way and provided with all the goods they might possibly have needed in a later life such as edible provisions in bowls, clothing, jewels and musical instruments. Everything was in perfect condition, including the naked mummies!

In one burial chamber there was a square-shaped drawing consisting of quadrangular signs, six by six, in four rows;

which could perhaps have been a copy of the "stone carpet" in the Assyrian palace at Nineveh. There were also strange sphinx-like figures with complicated horns on their heads and what Von Daniken takes to be wings on their backs, the postures of which suggested that they were struggling upwards to the skies.

But it is hardly possible to prove belief in a second and spiritual life from these Mongolian finds, as Von Daniken suggests. The deep-freeze methods of preservation suggested by the wood-lined and ice-filled chamber are too concerned with worldly purposes to suggest great interest in the after-life. It is difficult to understand why the Ancients thought that bodies prepared by them should have to satisfy certain conditions if resurrection was to take place, and for the present this is still an unresolved problem. So much though for Von Daniken's suggestion.

We too would like to know why the Scythians believed in a "resurrection", even if only a symbolic one, and why, like the Egyptians, they buried grave-goods for the after-life. We can only suggest that it may be due to some hereditary trait of the human mind. Is it something we are all born with, or something that has become fixed in our brains since time immemorial?

Thanks to the much appreciated co-operation of the Hermitage Museum in Leningrad, we can tell you the facts about the finds through the use of genuine photographs placed solely at our disposal.

Professor Sergei I. Rudenko unearthed a number of early Scythian graves at Pazarik in the High Altai Mountains in 1929. Listing these 2000-year-old graves in the order in which he found them, he gave them the names Kurgan 1, 2, 3, etc. His work was temporarily interrupted by the Second World War, but afterwards he took it up again. Each grave had been dug into the ground to a depth of about $4\frac{1}{2}$ metres, covered with timbers (plate 21) and topped with a mound made up of large numbers of stones (plate 20). The tomb is properly underground, but one would not really be justified in saying that it made use of a special deep-freeze technique; this was something Von Daniken could not know as he did not have access to the photographs and other details. The ice inside the chamber had originated as snow which had fallen on the outside of the tomb, melted in the summer, trickled through to the inside and finally become frozen again in the graves! It froze again almost immediately, since even in the summer the ground does not thaw out completely in this area. There were strong indications that tomb-robbers had gone down a shaft and reached the innermost graves to despoil them of their valuables, leaving the passage-way open after them, since there was no reason for them to fill it in. Snow and rain then penetrated down this shaft into the graves, where it froze and kept the bodies in good condition.

As we have seen, one of the best-known tombs was that of Kurgan V, which is mentioned by Von Daniken. After the removal of the mummies it was not entirely full of ice (plate 22). This tomb contained the bodies of a mummified man and woman which, in view of their age, were in very good order. But nobody looking at the photograph of the best-preserved mummy (plate 23) could imagine that it could ever be brought back to normal life again, especially in view of the fact that the brains and bowels had been taken out of the body, as we can see from the incisions made in it. It is strange that the Scythians knew and used the same techniques as the early Egyptians! Perhaps the source of the techniques was the same, namely the Ancients?

It seems very likely that the carpet-like drawing with the mysterious "signs and figures" on it was in fact a Persian carpet, which had been preserved so well that many of the colours remained (plate 24). This carpet is one of the oldest in the world and, as we have seen, at its centre there are some quadrangular signs, six by six and in four rows, which turn out to be plant motifs. Rather less clearly delineated are the horsemen, some of whom have their coats flapping open—it would not be difficult to imagine these to be wings, since these drawings are in general rather inferior! The sphinx-like shapes look like reindeer; and in the smallest drawings on the edge of the carpet there are deer and some sort of mountain goat, which is being attacked by a leopard or some other feline creature—but these will hardly be seen by the reader. Other tombs have contained similar pictures containing typically Scythian imagery, some of which are cut out of a kind of leather or felt.

To round off our discussion of mummies we must turn to the twentieth century variety. Extensive investigations into deep-freeze methods are being made and, particularly in America, a fairly large number of people—700 or so—have been mummified immediately after death and now await the future, deeply frozen in a kind of very expensive container. Their bodies differ from the Egyptian ones in being complete, and attempts to arrest decomposition have been entirely successful.

In both cases, Egyptian and modern alike, the actual cause of death will have to be removed before the "dead" can be brought back to life, a fact which is frequently forgotten! People die as the result of a physical defect, and it is just as important to be able to get rid of this mortal defect as it is to have the power of resurrection. Obviously this is quite impossible as far as the remains of the Egyptian mummies are concerned, and whether it will ever be practicable for the bodies in "deep-freeze" is a question for the *very* distant future! It is one that science will have to answer.

*   *   *

If one looks at the really mysterious figurines which have been found in Japan (fig. 22) it is not difficult to conclude that here we do indeed have reproductions, albeit faulty ones, of beings in a form of space-travel costume, and a number of authors have been at pains to use these objects to show that man . . . etc. You know what we mean. We have tried to explain these figurines in terrestrial terms, and this brought us after some detective work to the Jomon culture of Japan; they belong to the ancient cord pottery period—so named because woven rope patterns were the most commonly used form of decoration—which was developed by the forefathers of the Ainu, a race still existing in small numbers in Japan. Jomon civilization flourished from about the second millennium B.C. to roughly A.D. 300; it originated in Kiusju and Kansai (the area around Kioto), spreading farther north and west later on. These people seem to

127

have lived chiefly in huts which were rather peculiar in that they were partly underground, so that their houses were in fact covered pits. There are also some indications of cave-life

Japanese archaeologists divide the Jomon period into five successive stages. Their typical cordware art is met elsewhere in Northern Asia and Europe. The decoration is usually applied

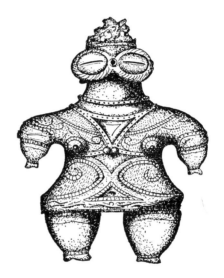

Fig. 22.

with a piece of wood or a cylindrical object wrapped in rope and then pressed into the soft clay, the granular imprint being quite clearly distinguishable on the pottery. In addition, wooden cylinders have been found containing incisions similar to the cord pattern. The edge of a scallop was also used, and sometimes bars of clay were fixed on. The decoration may well have had a practical reason: the clay was pressed to avoid any air bubbles being left inside, which would have caused the objects to break during the firing.

None of this has anything to do with space-travel costume, particularly as all the arms and legs of the figures are uncovered; a fact that is difficult to square with the needs of space-travel, for which the entire body must be protected.

The drawing of the figurine (fig. 22) most often referred to clearly depicts a female, as is usually the case. She has a broad

Fig. 23.

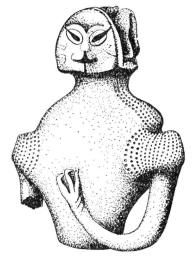

Fig. 24.　A Jomon
culture drawing, clearly
showing a feline being.

Fig. 25.　Another example
of Jomon cordware pottery.

129

face and neck, a heavily attired body, large oval eyes, a necklace, a Pompadour hair-style and a cord-patterned dress rolled up at her knees. Her strange eyes are strikingly suggestive of spectacles with oblique lenses, or even of parts of a space helmet. One must bear in mind that this was a Mongolian race when considering the artistic style, and this is reflected particularly strongly in the eyes of the figurines.

Figure 23 shows a similar eye-pattern, whereas in figure 24 —which is from the earliest Jomon period—we can see a feline development in the claws, the head and in particular the eyes. The transition stage dating from the middle period (fig. 25) also shows ringed, slit-like eyes. It may be that the eyes of the figurines dating from the last period are a stylized relic of the slanting cats' eyes we find on the figures produced in the earliest period.

There is a single statuette from the final period which has some kind of window instead of eyes, perhaps for defence against the sun, water or snow-glare. Although the limbs are uncovered, they could be taken to resemble those of astronauts!

# Chapter Eleven

Is the riddle of the megaliths solved?—how did the megalith builders emigrate?—Malta: perhaps the greatest
mystery in the Mediterranean?—an interim address to our
opponents.

Who is not familiar with the clusters of enormous stones at
Stonehenge in England and Carnac in France? Experts have
given them the name "megaliths"—"mega" being Greek for
"big" and "lithos" for "stone". The term is used for graves and
monuments, but in England numerous other expressions of
Celtic origin are employed: menhir, for instance, which is a
solitary standing-stone, the term coming from "maen" (stone)
and "hir" (long). A "dolmen" consists of two vertical menhirs
with a stone laid over the top, whereas a "cromlech" is a group
of menhirs and dolmens in varying patterns. Stonehenge,
therefore, is a cromlech.

Megaliths, burial-chambers and monuments occur in large
numbers in Europe and elsewhere; England has more than two
hundred cromlechs, and the number of burial-chambers in
Europe is around 45,000.

Unfortunately there has never been a complete review of this
fascinating subject, which has been studied only as far as special
aspects or sites are concerned. Perhaps the enormous area in
which megaliths can be found makes for difficulties in this
respect: they occur along the southern coasts of the Mediterranean and in Israel, Syria, Persia, India and Pakistan, frequently in large, localized groups in the latter countries.
Somewhat nearer home, they are to be found in Norway,
southern Sweden, Denmark, north-western Germany and along
the whole European coast into Spain, Portugal, Corsica,
Sardinia and Malta, as well as in the British Isles.

131

To develop our theories we must go somewhat farther into this matter and discuss the various characteristics and peculiarities of the megaliths. An enormous weight of stone was involved in the building of most of the burial-chambers and monuments. There are three main types of burial-chamber, and even when other forms seem to occur these prove to belong to one of the three groups.

The first type is distinguished by a corridor with rooms at the end, which are the actual burial-chambers. The second type has the same construction, but chambers may lead off from the corridor at the beginning. The third type is nothing more than a large stone box, which in most cases can only be inspected via the roof. A peculiar feature of the second group is that entrance is made either by means of a single stone hollowed out in the middle or by a cavity formed from two stones leaning against each other. This type of grave is thus appropriately called the "port-hole" type, and contrasts with the first group where the entrance is formed by two upright stones with another large one in front, which could be rolled away in case of need. It is a common feature of the first group to find square, oval or round chambers whereas the second has almost exclusively rectangular ones.

All three types of grave can be found singly or in clusters, and all are generally protected by a heap of stones and surrounded by a wall that was originaly 50–130 cm. wide. The wall is often heart-shaped, its broadest part enclosing at the widest part of the tomb.

All the graves contained large numbers of skeletons, often in disordered piles—a sign that the tombs had been in use for a long time, and that bones from earlier burials had simply been pushed aside to make room for others. Remains of pigs, deer, cows, sheep, horses, dogs and other animals were frequently found inside as well, plus flint implements such as spearheads, axes, knives and pieces of earthenware. It is curious how the "spirit" has gone out of these artefacts once they have been broken up; and it is odd that metal implements from the first age of metalworking have not been found, since this age was contemporaneous with the megalith builders. Of course metal tools have been unearthed, but they are either of a much more recent date or they must belong to a culture that was aware of the existence of metal at this period and was able to use it. It is all the odder because although the megalith builders knew about copper and bronze they did not use these metals to dress the stone but kept instead to stone tools. These included many very heavy stone hammers; the technique employed was very much like that of the Egyptians, for instance, who produced their granite obelisks with similar stone hammers even though they too had been familiar for a long time with copper and bronze.

Several people have suggested that the megalith builders had religious reasons for not using metal tools, and this may well be correct in view of the absence of other explanations and considering what has actually been found. What is important is the strange coincidence that all the megaliths, everywhere, have been made exclusively with stone tools!

The megaliths which have been studied in most detail are those of England and France, and they can be taken as typical. In both cases it seems that the peoples who first inhabited these areas could not have constructed the cromlechs, the best proof of which is the fact that those buildings they were in fact responsible for are very much older than the megaliths. The early inhabitants showed no inclination to develop along the lines of the megalith builders or to create special techniques for the building of their prehistoric constructions.

The English megaliths were built chiefly in the second millennium B.C., at a time when the people there lived mainly by hunting, although it has recently been established that they knew a certain amount about agriculture and stockbreeding. History provides no examples of hunting peoples of this kind building monuments comparable to the megaliths, but it is very likely that after the sudden disappearance of the race who *did* build them, the surviving peoples continued to use them for their own ends, which were probably chiefly religious in character. It has even been shown that the monuments were actually extended, but where this was done the methods employed were quite different from those employed by the original builders.

Who were the original builders and where did they come from? Many experts, including prominent archaeologists, believe that they were a trading race. Fine: but where there is trade there must be goods for exchange, and we would like to know what these megalith builders brought with them.

But apart from that it is difficult to imagine that merchants living abroad would go to the trouble or, still more important, have enough time to build such burial-chambers and monuments. Those articles which have been found in the graves belong with few exceptions to the resident peoples whom the megalith builders were visiting; and no objects representative of the megalith builders have been found except perhaps for the tools used in building the megaliths—and these have not been found in such large numbers to make it likely that they were used for trade. We have grave doubts about the "trading theory", all the more so since the accompanying evidence is virtually nil.

After weighing up all the available evidence very carefully we believe that the megalith builders came from Malta, and they were nothing less than the missionaries of a cult which had spread from that island to cover an enormous area.

Megaliths in their original and oldest form are found in Malta! To reach other areas where megaliths are found it was vitally necessary to build sea-worthy ships, and there is no doubt that at the time when these cromlechs were built there was not *one* but several races in the Mediterranean area who were perfectly capable of constructing reliable, sea-going ships: one needs only to think of the Egyptians and the Cretans.

However, there is no evidence that such boats were constructed in Malta at that time, so we must assume that the missionaries—if we may so call them—made use of shipping from other cultural centres in the Mediterranean. The outline of a Mycenaean dagger on one of the stones at Stonehenge points in this direction.

As early as about 3000 B.C. Malta must have been known throughout the whole Mediterranean area as a cult centre, and as such it would have had contacts with almost all the other civilizations in those regions; and there are even strong indications that a number of oracles lived on Malta and were consulted by, for example, the Egyptians!

In ancient times religious rites and trade often went hand in hand, so it might well be that merchants came from other Mediterranean districts, or even beyond, to visit the island and then took missionaries with them on their travels. This would be an acceptable explanation of some of the metals and other artefacts found which indicate commerce between numerous races over large areas. Moreover, some of these finds date from a time when these peoples had no sea-going ships of their own, so the objects in question must have been transported to the places in which they were eventually discovered by someone who *did* possess such craft. But one must be careful here since, being so few, the artefacts can hardly be considered as objects of trade, nor are they typical of the megalith builders!

There is one important piece of evidence in support of the theory that missionaries travelled by sea-going vessels, which is that with one exception the megaliths are found by the coasts in exposed situations and on islands accessible *solely* by boat. The megalith builders have left behind no artefacts suggesting that they themselves constructed ships, which reinforces the conclusion that they made use of the vessels, and probably the crews, of other civilizations.

Scandinavian battle-axes found in Spain, together with iron spearheads unearthed in Scandinavia which date from long before the widespread use of iron, are some of the things which indicate that there must have been trade over great distances.

As we have said two of the most interesting and the best studied megalith sites are Stonehenge, which lies along the Avon in an area between Cornwall and Wales, and Carnac in Brittany.

Stonehenge consists of a large number of intricately placed stones originally forming the shapes of a circle and a horseshoe, with a diameter of about 115 metres. The whole thing is surrounded by a dyke, but there is an entrance to the monument itself. Its alignment is of little account apart from three important menhirs, the innermost of which is called the "altar", the central one the slaughter stone, while the block set up outside the actual monument is known as the heel stone. These three are set in a single line and are so arranged that the sun rises above the heel stone on June 21st of every year with a small deviation.

The first researches into the purpose and structure of Stonehenge seem to have taken place in the seventeenth century, when James I requested his architect Inigo Jones to undertake an investigation; but since no modern techniques were available at that time, it was decided that the stones were simply the remains of a Roman temple.

There was little research of any importance for a long time after this, and it was not until our own century that further work revealed, in 1954, that this ancient monument originated in the dim and distant past long before our era. Yet even these investigations were largely a matter of surmise and included some extremely dubious theories. The "Druid Theory" is an amusing one that is worth recalling, since the Druids have often been mentioned in history books. About 200 B.C. Sotion of Alexandria referred to the Druids in his writings as the philosophers of the Celts. Julius Caesar also described them, but as he found them in France rather than in England. Writing in 50 B.C., he tells us how he saw the Druids acting as priests and judges. They had an independent organization over and above the tribal system, and they were headed by an Archdruid. They met once a year in the neighbourhood of Chartres.

Writing in about 61 B.C., Tacitus describes the English Druids in much the same way, and there are vague Irish and Welsh legends which claim that they were in existence until the introduction of Christianity.

A good many people, including some experts, are convinced that the Druids built Stonehenge, forgetting the enormous time-span between the Druids of Julius Caesar's era and that of the actual megalith builders—a matter of some eighteen hundred years!

It is generally agreed that Stonehenge was erected in three

stages between 1850 and 1700 B.C. The first phase consisted of the erection of the large stones by the original megalith builders; the second was an extension of the work done in the first, and is ascribed to the Bell-beaker Folk; and the third was carried out by the original inhabitants of the area. It was not until the American scholar Hawkins came on the scene that any further conclusions could be drawn.

Fig. 26. Stonehenge

Gerald S. Hawkins, a professor of astronomy at Boston University, is an eminent scientist with a number of excellent works to his credit. Some years ago he was sent to Larkhill, fairly near Stonehenge. He was much impressed by Stonehenge and was so taken with the fact that on June 21st the sun rises exactly above the heel stone that he undertook a detailed and extensive investigation. He began by collecting all the available information possible, and in typical American fashion he used a computer (which he nicknamed Oscar) to deal with the enormous amount of detail he amassed. Having fed Oscar with all the Stonehenge data together with material about the sun, moon and stars, he anxiously awaited the outcome. The computer's conclusion was totally unexpected. Oscar proved decisively that Stonehenge had been built as a huge observatory for following the movements of the sun and moon, and the same result was given after Hawkins conclusively tested the computer's findings. By using the figures supplied by the computer he was able to assess the age of the first megaliths independently of the views of other experts, together with data about the various eclipses from that period to the present day! The Hawkins theory is already several years old, and many of the experts who have studied it acknowledge its validity. It can be said that one of history's enigmas has been solved with the help of the most modern equipment.

*    *    *

As the crow flies, the distance between Stonehenge and Brittany is not too great, and there we can find another interesting collection of megaliths which are similar in every respect to Stonehenge.

The so-called "alignments" are typical of Brittany. These consist of avenues of stones of varying sizes which usually end in megalith circles or other shapes, and point in the same direction as the three Stonehenge menhirs! This was discovered, not by another Hawkins, but by a Frenchman, Major Devoir. Can such alignments be due to chance, bearing in mind the evidence of Stonehenge? It seems unlikely: we believe these monuments, together with other megaliths, are a kind of gigantic calendar for fixing the dates of certain religious periods or special days in the year.

Although not all such monuments were necessarily burial-places, remains have often been found under the large stones in most areas, and these deposits were placed in the foundations before the stones were erected. Probably they had a magical and religious significance.

As elsewhere, the stones in Brittany were dressed exclusively by means of stone implements; and here too there are three types of graves. Again, enormous stones were used; in every respect they strongly resemble other megaliths, and Stonehenge in particular.

In passing it is worth mentioning the weight and the exceptional measurements of some of the stones. In a grave at Bagneux near Saumur there is a stone 18·6 metres long and 5 metres wide, while a lintel stone from the same tomb is estimated to weigh eighty-six tons. Carnac has the largest of all known megaliths, but it is lying on the ground, broken into five pieces. This stone was originally more than twenty metres high and weighed 347 tons—347,000 kilos! The builders must have had techniques unknown to us to achieve with their simple tools feats which would be almost impossible today; and this kind of skill is not something one would expect to find among the original inhabitants of the megalith areas, who were then living in the Stone Age!

*     *     *

In the course of excavations over the last few decades it has been ascertained that around 3000 B.C. Malta was the flourishing centre of a cult which has no equal even in later history.

Malta—or Melite, according to St Paul—became independent in 1965 for the first time in its extremely long history. With the smaller islands of Gozo, Comino and Filfla, it is all that remains of a land bridge which, it is assumed, connected present-day Italy and Africa until about 100,000 years ago. Various remains have been found of extinct types of dwarf elephants, hippopotamus and deer. The anthropologist Arthur Keith found eight human teeth, together with the fossil remains of a dwarf hippopotamus, in the Grotto of Darkness at Ghar Dalan, near the capital city, Valletta. Keith is convinced that two of these teeth belonged to a Neanderthal man who lived, as we have seen, from about 110,000 to 30,000 years ago. This discovery means that Malta has been populated for over 30,000 years!

This island has always lain on important shipping routes, and conceals a large number of secrets, most of which are still shrouded in mystery. The history of Malta reaches back further than 3000 B.C., judging by the discoveries made there, but its prehistory is still a matter of speculation.

The religious cult which was centred on Malta is also a matter of debate. Some experts maintain that it must have been a sun-cult in view of the artefacts that have been discovered, and a fairly complex one at that; but the number and nature of the proofs they provide are not convincing. What is certain is that there must have been oracles living on Malta who were well-known throughout the whole Mediterranean area, and that the cult was complicated in structure.

There are so many enormous stones left over from monuments and tombs in Malta and the smaller islands that one is justified in thinking that the settlements must once have looked like a kind of New York of antiquity. There are also types of dolmen which can be found elsewhere in Europe; in fact the similarities in building techniques to megaliths beyond Malta are very considerable, the only difference being that here they are much older!

The hypogeum, a subterranean vault at Hal Saflieni, is fairly well known, as are the temples of Tarxien and Mnaidra. It consists of a large number of rooms, corridors and hollowed out rocks, which give one the illusion of being in a megalith burial-chamber of huge stones, so well have the builders achieved their effects. Equally striking are the spiral decorations, which were done with red ochre, a material often used in prehistoric art.

The splendid acoustics of the hypogeum are something of a puzzle, suggesting that a mysterious technique was used, since it cannot be accidental that every word can be heard echoing from vault to vault, quite clearly in even the smallest chambers. It seems very likely that it was in use as an oracular shrine during the earliest phase.

Later on, probably at the end of the Stone Age, the hypogeum was used as a huge burial-chamber, for all the rooms were found to have been filled with red earth (pipe-clay). Over 7000 skeletons were found in this pipe-clay, and the excavators were immediately impressed by the almost complete absence of any long bones: a sign that the bodies of the deceased must have remained outside the hypogeum for a long time before being put there in an advanced state of decomposition.

Although this custom is well-known elsewhere, there may be quite a different explanation. Could it be that the leading missionaries who died abroad were brought back to Malta? If true, this would explain the absence of nearly all the long bones!

And there are other similarities, which cannot be purely a matter of chance. We have mentioned the fact that the oldest megaliths are to be found in Malta, and we have indicated the similarities of building techniques, stone-dressing methods, and so on.

But there is still more to come! In Tarxien, Hal Saflieni and Hagiar Kim we find a curious spiral decoration, which can also be found at great distances from Malta—for example, on the large stone at the entrance to one of the greatest of all megalith graves in New Grange, Ireland (fig. 27), and on other tombs in Scandinavia and Brittany. The Frenchman Dechelette sees this pattern as representing the eyes of some female divinity from

140

the Stone Age, which at first took the form of concentric circles but were later represented as linked spirals. The similarities are very striking, notwithstanding the great distances between the various sites. Moreover the sites themselves are alike, whether in Malta or in other places where great stones lie in front of the temples and tombs; our three drawings shown indicate these affinities.

Fig. 27.
New Grange

Hagiar Kim

Tarxien

It is not only this decorative motif that suggests evidence of contact between the Mediterranean and remote places. In July 1953 a number of drawings on some of the large menhirs at Stonehenge were discovered by chance one day when the sun was going down. They were not scratched on, as was the custom about 18,000 years ago in the Magdalenian period, but had been struck out of the rock, which presupposes the use of axes and daggers. The dagger employed was of a type chiefly used at that time in Crete and the Mycaenean kingdom; however in view of the frequent intercourse between these different areas, it must have been known in Malta too. The English archaeologist

141

Crawford rightly states that this type of dagger was unknown in Britain at that time and, he adds, no native would have drawn a picture of a dagger quite alien to him. For this reason, and for others which are too detailed to mention here, he presumes that representatives of a Mediterranean civilization must have been present when the first phase of Stonehenge was being built around 1850 B.C. Moreover in almost every district in which megaliths occur we come across accompanying drawings of axes, daggers, ships and so forth—as for instance, at the passage-grave of Mané Lud in Locmariaquer which was discovered by René Galles, or the tombs of north-western Germany; and eight similar sketches have been found on stone slabs from the Kivik tomb in southern Sweden (fig. 28).

In earlier times there must have been many more drawings on the megaliths but changes in the temperature, the rain and wind, and moulds and mosses have all resulted in their gradual obliteration; only in few cases did they manage to remain visible. However it has only recently been discovered during the course of excavations that those parts that were under the soil now retained some signs which had not gone to ruin.

Again, large numbers of stone balls were found during some excavations in Malta. They were of varying sizes and it may be that they had some religious significance or that they were used in transporting the great stone boulders. Similar stone balls have been unearthed on other sites where megaliths have been built; one more piece of evidence to add to the list of objects resembling each other from different parts of the world!

Naturally the great stones of the megaliths were put in place without the help of bull-dozers, cranes and so on. This becomes clear when we examine, for example, the pyramids of Egypt, the Baalbek remains in the Lebanon, or the old temples of Peru and Mexico. Time and again one comes across huge fragments of stone weighing tens of thousands of kilos—or even, as in the case of the terraces at Baalbrek, around two million kilos—which must have been brought over long distances and then placed together without the aid of any kind of cement, so exactly that one cannot even push a razor-blade between the joins. This kind of precision is almost impossible to achieve today, and leads us to a question which, though persistently evaded by modern science, must nonetheless be asked, namely, what sort of technical skills did the Ancients possess, skills such as *we* cannot aspire to, and what was the source of their knowledge? In spite of all our achievements we cannot match the achievements of

Fig. 28. The eight stone slabs from the Kivik tomb, Southern Sweden.

these ancient civilizations, and today we appear to be actually slipping down the ladder.

*　　*　　*

There are two points we would like to make at this stage which will, to some extent, take the wind out of our opponents' sails.

First of all, there is the question of stone-dressing by means of stone tools alone. Many people will point out that traces of copper have been found on several stones in England and France. To this we would reply that such traces are accidental: they occur in such minute amounts that they provide no proof of the general use of copper or bronze tools. After the departure of the megalith builders the stone circles were used for mainly religious purposes, and when copper came into use objects made of this metal were buried in the vicinity. Copper was even used to make drawings and signs, but these are clearly quite different from—and much more recent than—the earlier ones. Even today tourists use a metal implement when they want to scratch their initials or some other sign on the megaliths, and surely no one would consider their drawings and scribblings the work of the megalith builders? And yet the megaliths are covered with such drawings!

Secondly, you may ask why there should be three types of grave, if they were all constructed by one and the same race? Is it not more likely that if the builders had come from Malta they would have known only *one* type of tomb! This is a strong argument, but once again a useful comparison can be drawn between ancient and modern times. Take our own Christian rites, for example. Rightly or wrongly, we call ourselves Christians and profess the same ceremonies in the main—and yet we are divided between Catholics, Protestants, Calvinists and other

144

sects. We build different types of churches and bury our dead in varying styles of grave: communal graves, individual, mausoleums, family vaults, etc. Similarly, there is no reason at all why this should not have been the case in ancient times too, when the megaliths were built.

The megalith builders had a complicated system of religious ceremony, but it must certainly have had room for various forms of worship. It is possible that three sects left Malta to spread "the faith" over a huge area; each sect probably sent its own missionaries and those who died when abroad, would have been buried according to the custom of their particular sect. One must bear in mind that the stone-dressing was done in the same way for all the burial-chambers, that the material used was the same and that the construction styles shared the same features; and the decorative art forms shared a common identity. Bearing all this in mind, it becomes clear that there were three "streams" of megalithic culture and that it was by no means created by unrelated peoples, as is sometimes believed in England and France.

By now you may agree with us that megalithic culture spread from the Mediterranean regions and, in particular, from Malta. The stone balls, the strange art-forms, the absence of merchandise, the presence of stone tools only, the similarities in building and burial methods, the remains found under the large stones and the building of the huge monuments for calendar purposes, all support this theory—and make matters rather more difficult for our opponents. But even though we may have succeeded in lifting a corner of the veil of mystery which lies over the megaliths, we are well aware that at least as many new problems have arisen or have been left unsolved.

For example, the sudden disappearance of the megalith builders is still an enigma. They appear to have stopped work quite abruptly without leaving us any useful clues as to their reasons. Nor do we know where they came from in the first place. From whom did they obtain the knowledge that was indispensable for the transport and construction of the massive rocks? Above all, how did they acquire the knowledge needed for the

Fig. 29.  Sillustani megalith circles in Peru, with similarities to the so-called Cretan shaft-graves.

construction of the solar observatory? We could go on asking such questions for ever!

And there are countless questions to be asked if we turn to the even more impressive and enigmatic megaliths of Peru. Megaliths have been found on the Sillustani peninsula near Umayo (fig. 29) and, as at Stonehenge, we find an altar, a slaughter stone and a heel stone! The similarities are really quite amazing and the implications are enough to make one's head reel.

Could it be that, apart from spreading over Scandinavia, Europe, the Mediterranean, Central Asia and India, the megalith builders reached South America long before anyone else? We are not yet completely certain that this is the case, but it could well be that in the near future we shall have to re-write our history all over again!

When talking about the Ancients, we may be referring to the oldest civilization in the world from which all other cultures

146

have derived. Did it provide the inspiration for the megalith builders, whose culture in any case reaches back beyond 3000 B.C.? We may one day know when and if this original culture flourished, and this brings us back to the main theme of this book: how was it possible that simple Stone Age farmers, nomads and hunters should, after tens of thousands of years of a wandering life, suddenly evince an appreciable and hitherto inexplicable urge to achieve a higher and more sophisticated culture and standard of living? Are we dealing here with the descendants of the Ancients and their religion? Did they form a "religious sect" which was thousands of years old and which retained only the memories of earlier times?

We would like to conclude this chapter with a word to those who will no doubt violently attack our theories. As late as the nineteen-fifties there were still many people, including some famous scholars, who considered space-travel completely impossible. They even tried to "prove" that they were in the right. Weightlessness was claimed to be fatal, and the idea of people landing on the moon was dismissed as something that belonged to the realms of science fiction. You may well smile at this, but people seriously believed that such ideas were correct: yet by now our attitudes have changed to such an extent that an Apollo space flight, with astronauts carrying out a lunar landing, often goes ignored on our television screens—we switch to another, more popular event or programme. The front pages of our newspapers no longer carry headlines about astronauts— and the sceptics of the nineteen-fifties have almost completely vanished!

# PART THREE

# Footsteps along the Path of Science

# Chapter Twelve

Microcosm and macrocosm—what might have happened if an extra-terrestrial intelligence had discovered our planet in prehistoric times?—has man an inbuilt urge to destroy himself?

We would like you for a moment to forget what you have read so far to consider the fact that if one looks up at the skies on a clear evening one can see an enormous number of heavenly bodies, some of which may be recognizable from the patterns they form, such as the Great Bear, the Little Bear, the Pole Star and Orion.

Astronomy is the science with which we investigate the nature of the universe and in recent years it seems to have been on the threshold of an adventure the like of which has never previously been experienced. Space-travel is a part of this experience, and is advancing at great speed. As we have seen, twenty years ago some people still did not believe in the possibility of space-travel and lunar landings were thought to be absurd. Today such things may not be exactly daily events, and they can still attract the necessary attention; but in a few years' time they will be overshadowed by still more striking achievements, and lunar journeys will be treated as a matter of course. Perhaps they are already taken *too* much for granted; do we really appreciate what we are doing? The first moon journey can be seen as the opening stage in the conquest of the universe—a universe which is revealing itself even more clearly as the greatest mystery that has ever existed. Nobody ever suspected the presence of quasars and pulsars, and although we are still a long way from knowing exactly what they involve, they do nonetheless feature frequently in the thinking of modern astronomy.

Fig. 30

In this way, science slowly advances; almost every year discovers new phenomena. But can man spiritually assimilate his findings about the universe? Such questions should be asked, since to answer them incorrectly might well prove fatal for mankind.

All thinking persons, including scientists, seriously consider the possibility of their being intelligent life elsewhere in the universe. Although the term "intelligent life" is inadequate, we prefer it to the much more frequently used expression "extra-terrestrial civilization". After all, who can say that what we consider civilized life in fact provides a useful or valid criterion for the whole universe?

There is an enormous increase of interest in science fiction literature, and one might well ask if this kind of writing is not in some ways proof that human beings, consciously or unconsciously, recognize the existence of other intelligent forms of life in the universe.

The number of stars, planets and solar systems is infinite and unimaginably large. The estimated number has increased steadily through the centuries, and it may be that the chances that life exists elsewhere have likewise increased. It seems virtually inevitable that *Homo sapiens* may one day meet his cosmic counterparts: and this would mean the end of human evolution as it has been conditioned by the world we live in . . . or the final end of man himself. Only a very few people have ever grasped this and they have been considered men of genius, because they were far in advance of their contemporaries in taking such possibilities seriously.

Albert Einstein was one of them; we still do not know just how much we owe to him. His theory about the universe, which was based on Riemann's idea of curved space, postulated that the universe was finite and space curved, and that space shrinks and expands to cosmic pulses. This pulsating universe is built up from an unimaginable number of components; to our eyes these components seem gigantic in size, but they are themselves constructed out of other, smaller ones. For example, a solar system consists of one or more stars with its planets, each of which moves along its orbit according to fixed laws which must exist even if nothing else does. But each part of a solar system has in its turn smaller constituents: a planet like our own world is made of minerals and so forth, which are themselves made up of yet smaller particles—and so the process goes on until we reach the microcosmic world.

It was centuries before the molecule was discovered, after which it was for a long time thought to be the smallest particle in existence. But then the atom was discovered, and before long this too was found to be divisible into smaller units—protons, neutrons and electrons. The latter move around the nucleus of an atom, apparently subject to the same laws as those that dictate the path of planets around the sun.

But these discoveries were merely a beginning! Now the existence of even tinier particles has been confirmed: such as leptons, light and heavy mesons and hyperons which again—as you may guess?—can be broken down further.

In 1954 the existence of antineutrons was established—particles which are negatively charged and can cancel out others. When Nobel prizewinner P.A.M. Dirac published his theory of the "negative charge" in 1928, he was taken for a crank, yet today every scholar accepts his findings. Might it not be that both microcosm and macrocosm are subject to identical laws and are constructed on the same principles? It is only one step from Dirac's theory to the hypothesis that "antimatter" exists in the universe! And from there to discover that the only important factor is time!

At some stage the microcosm and the macrocosm must overlap, or at least meet—an astonishing thought, since it would mean that man himself is a microcosm in the universe and one of its lowliest parts, and always will be.

Inside us is the infinitely small, outside us the immeasurably huge; both recognize similar laws and the same principles of construction, but where is the meeting-point between them?

The transition from matter to energy and *vice versa* in microcosm and macrocosm might be an explanation of Einstein's pulsating universe. Numerous scholars have put forward the notion that there are anti-worlds, anti-atoms and even anti-beings, and scientific progress appears to confirm such theories. The Dutch physicist Piket has even developed a theory—like Dirac's—that we can perceive only a part of cosmic phenomena: they are perceptible only so long as they are not in a state of balance or equilibrium, and when the positive and negative charges are in equilibrium the particles are imperceptible. Whether he is right or wrong is a matter of debate; we can only hope that man has enough time left to ascertain the truth of this and many other theories. In this connection, any contact with an extra-terrestrial intelligence would be fatal: we just do not know *what* to expect upon any such initial confrontation.

Imagine, as some writers do, that prehistoric man had encountered an extra-terrestrial intelligence; what might have taken place? It may be that the being from outer space *was* faced with a creature "capable of reaching the stars"; but a *very* long time was to elapse before this ever took place, and only now are we engaged upon what we can properly call the conquest of space.

Any extra-terrestrial intelligence able to undertake space journeys—maybe even at an interstellar level—would inevitably have realized this, and would have taken measures to deal with it in advance. But we must not automatically assume that the being from space would have been recognized as "human" by primitive man or his ancestors; and neither must we assume that the extra-terrestrial intelligences would have treated mankind in a similar fashion, since our own earthly criteria would not necessarily apply to other inhabitants of the universe!

Did the extra-terrestrial intelligence discern the real threat to the future represented by man at this confrontation—if it ever took place? Did they realize what a lust for conquest man would display once he started his conquest of space? And if they did, what did they do at the time to prevent it? Can a logical solution be found to this question?

We know today that the human mind can be influenced in a number of ways: by light, sound, chemical substances, suggestion and hypnosis. Advertisers are a good example, since they are constantly devising new methods to condition us to buy their goods or use their services. Everybody is influenced by advertisements throughout his life; an example of advertising techniques from America was used to promote the sale of a well-known brand of cigarettes while a film was being shown; material boosting the qualities of that particular brand was very briefly flashed on to the screen and though the flashes were so short as to be imperceptible to the conscious mind, the message still got across to those watching the film. A cigarette booth was installed at the exit and the only brands offered were those advertised during the film-show. In less than ten minutes the entire stock had been sold, in spite of the fact that many of the purchasers had never bought that particular brand before. This little example, taken from a host of others, illustrates how easily a human being can be influenced.

An extra-terrestrial intelligence could have decided without any difficulty to subject man to some kind of posthypnotic suggestion or instruction which would ensure that he would be unable in his present state to set about the conquest of space. It could even be that this conditioning was of an extremely malignant nature: man's "inbuilt urge to destroy himself" might have been imparted to him at that time, even though its ultimate manifestation was meant to occur once he had achieved the potential for conquering the universe. If we look around us today it has to be admitted that such conditioning, which may perhaps have been repeated at fixed intervals by the extra-terrestrial beings, could not have produced more effective results!

Man's impulse to self-destruction on a large scale began when the first rocket experiments were made with the ultimate aim of making lunar landings possible. These experiments took place in Germany before and during our first large-scale attempt at "self-destruction", the Second World War. The first A1 and A2 rockets were built in Germany, and made to function almost perfectly, and these were followed by the notorious V1 and V2 rockets.

How strange it is that the first genuine attempts at space-travel—and thus at mastering the universe—should have been accompanied by threats to life here in this world and not to living matter out in space! Atom and hydrogen bombs, poison gases, biological and chemical warfare and so on were developed almost simultaneously with all kinds of material that would be needed for space. Now that we have reached the moon, we know only too well that we can destroy ourselves. Nor are we threatened only by the weapons we have made, for we have created a number of other ways of destroying ourselves, such as pollution in its widest sense. Water and air pollution are the most dangerous, and both are increasing daily if not hourly. Then there is the drastic increase in the number of fatal traffic accidents throughout the world, caused by the vehicles travelling at ever increasing speeds—which ensures that survival from collisions is less and less likely. And the individual often does his best to destroy himself, for example, by the increased use of drugs and alcohol.

Even the oceans, our last hope and the ultimate source of life, are being seriously polluted by mankind's self-destructive urge. Every day all over the world tankers clean out their holds with sea-water, and hundreds of tons of chemical waste are dumped in the sea. Enormous patches of oil were seen floating on the Atlantic Ocean when Thor Heyerdahl made his Ra expeditions, and these are lethal to most forms of marine life that come into contact with them. In the summer months we even have to swim in oily water which has been ruthlessly polluted by our fellow creatures. To us it is merely a nuisance: but to nature it is deadly. We pollute our rivers, and thus our drinking water, to such an extent that, for example, the Scheldt in Holland no longer has any living organisms in it; this means that it is unable to purify itself any more, so it becomes "dead" water which then pours into the North Sea along with all its waste products. A number of chemical firms have been compelled to devise different methods of waste-disposal. In the so-called "deep well method", the waste is buried two hundred metres or more under the ground through a network of pipes; it is then out of sight and can no longer cause annoyance, yet this method carries with it still greater risks because nobody knows exactly how the ground is stratified at this depth or whether harmful chemical wastes might not eventually find a way through other rock beds to pollute our drinking water. Long-term pollution on the cheap best describes this particular method!

As if this were not enough, there is the danger of the world becoming over-populated. As it is, life cannot be maintained in the most heavily populated areas; we must ask ourselves how long we can go on living like this, and how long life can go on functioning more or less normally in the event of serious calamities like war, particularly if shipping is brought to a standstill and it becomes impossible to import everything we need. How long could we keep going? Would it be a matter of days or weeks before we were without fuel and food?

The Dutch government, like governments everywhere, provides a partial answer to the problem. Dutch farmers are obliged to register the sale or purchase of all cattle, as well as the birth and death of every animal. The total cattle stock would have to be drawn upon as a last resort in a time of emergency—but what happens after that?

We can only hope that our apparent urge to exterminate ourselves is not an affliction that was laid upon us by an extra-terrestrial intelligence, however eagerly some writers may believe this to be the case. If our self-destructive urge springs from within man himself we can still hope that something may be done before darkness overtakes intelligent life on earth!

# Chapter Thirteen

Why did men bury the dead in prehistoric times?—why did
they begin to build?—civilization on an island?—how must
things have seemed at the time?

Why man buries his dead relatives is a question which all of us
ask at some time or other, and various theories have been put
forward to provide an answer. Some people believe that the
custom was developed for religious reasons; another and more
likely theory suggests that it resulted from a feeling of piety
and the wish to ensure that the body of the deceased was not
eaten up by animals in the vicinity—and this sense of piety
is one of the basic differences between man and the animals. It
may be the same instinct that urges the new-born child to drink
its mother's milk also persuaded prehistoric man to bury his
dead, and that the answer lies in a combination of these theories.

There are many other such questions. What, for example, is
the meaning of the mysteries of birth, life and death? We know
a great deal about these processes—and we can understand
scientifically how they come about—yet we know next to nothing about why they do so.

Science cannot simulate even the simplest of our organs with
complete efficiency; we are so complex that we contain within
ourselves another enigma of which science knows nothing,
namely the human spirit—the only part of ourselves that is not
confined to the world of space and time. Man's spirit is not
constricted by the laws that govern physical bodies, yet we know
virtually nothing about it, despite the fact that we are gaining
an increasingly better idea of the almost limitless possibilities
of the human brain.

We are often told about such phenomena as parapsychology,
clairvoyance, spiritualism and so on, all of which contain a

measure of truth; yet because we are ignorant of their under-
lying principles we regrettably tend to reject evidence of their
validity as defective or inadequate, and we do so because we fail
to realize that we do so through our own lack of insight and in-
ability to understand the truth that lies behind everything. We
are unable to overcome our own shortcomings in this respect.

Yet despite this, considerable developments are being made
in the vital sciences of psychology and psychiatry, together with
their related disciplines. Though one should not indulge in
prophecies, it may be that the dreams of the alchemists will one
day be realized; the human mind will become the master of
matter, and man's spiritual progress will equal—or, better
still, control—the progress he has made in the technological
field.

In the past man has always been able to dominate his environment and protect himself against the dangers around him
to some extent. At first he hid behind overhanging rocks or
lived in caves; but driven by necessity to follow and hunt animals in open terrain, he soon began to erect the first primitive
huts in order to have a roof over his head, even though the
earliest of these were little more than covered pits. Man made
himself somewhere to live, partly for protection against roaming
animals and partly for shelter from inclement weather.

The life of a hunter was of necessity a nomadic one, and this
was a handicap to man's further growth, since so much time
had to be spent moving around; often there was not enough time
left over for farming, of which there was little. Great distances
often had to be covered; as we have seen, there is a theory that
the Americas were populated by tribal movements from Asia via
the Bering Strait, then still a land bridge, and that these tribes
were following the migration of cold-climate animals. Everything points to the fact that the evolution of mankind and his
forebears was a very gradual process, and that a period of ten
thousand years or more was hardly of any importance.

But we should ask ourselves whether civilization may not
have first arisen on a large, fertile island? If the island had a
great deal of wild life which was unable to move about and

Plates 16 and 17.  Glozel.

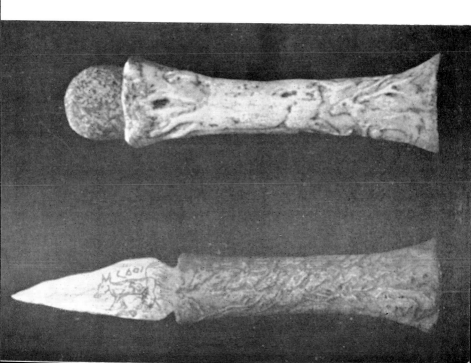

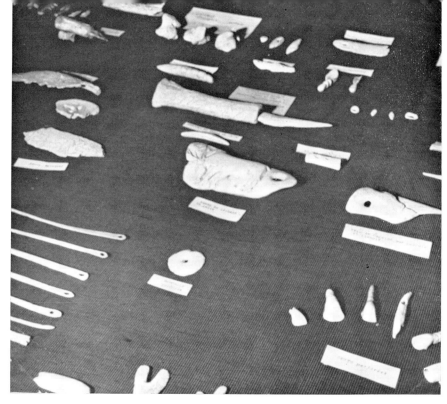

Plate 18. Some of the Glozel bone remains.

Plate 19. Glozel.

Plate 20.   Burial-mound of Kurgan V at Pazarik before
it was opened.

Plate 21.   A view of the same after partial levelling-off.
One can clearly see the roofing of tree-trunks
protecting the grave deep under the field.

Plate 22. Tomb of Kurgan V, partly filled with ice. The two coffins made from tree-trunks are clearly visible after removal of the mummies.

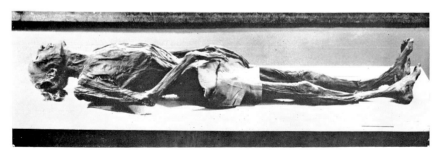

Plate 23. The best preserved mummy from the same tomb. Underneath the diaphragm the rough incision tightly sewn together after removal of the inner organs can clearly be seen.

Plate 24. The so-called "Persian carpet" from the
tomb of Kurgan V. In the middle there are clearly made
symbols: four rows with six in each.

Plate 25.   The best-known of the Piri Reis maps.

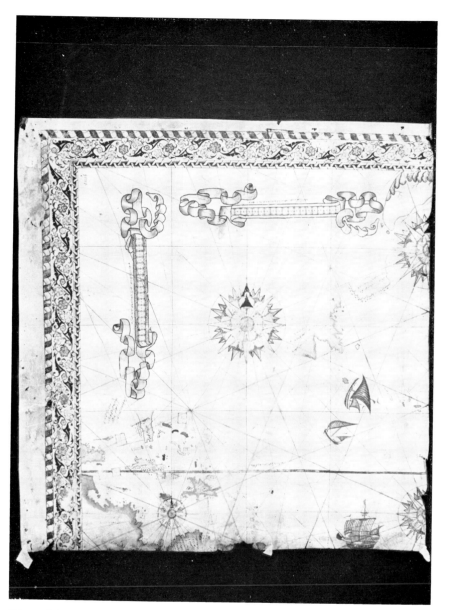

Plate 26.   The so-called second Piri Reis chart.

Plate 27. The Glareanus map dating from 1510. It
clearly shows the elongated shape of South America,
with both east and west coasts. (Photo J. Sluimer)

compel men to travel great distances in order to follow it, and if it had a luxuriant vegetation with a good supply of edible fruits and a favourable climate, is it not in fact probable that mankind would have developed here earlier than on the mainland?

This is a question which deserves an affirmative answer, particularly if the island had a *very* mild climate. On the mainland the nomadic hunter could only have formed large-scale communities very gradually, since he had to be able to ensure an abundance of food, and very often his farming and his environment were too poor. But on an island a race could have developed almost unmolested once protection from dangerous animals had been assured, and the island people would have been helped by climatic advantages, fertile soil, good flora and fauna with a limited means of expansion.

Has such an island ever existed? Almost certainly!

Greenland is an example: about 12,000 years ago it had an extremely favourable climate. Although research would be very difficult, it would cause a good deal of surprise if it could be proved that a prehistoric civilization had existed there.

But we need not confine ourselves to Greenland, since such islands can be found all over the world, even in places with unfavourable climates today which seem to have little in common with the type of island we have in mind. Is there any evidence to support this theory? Indeed there is, and in the next chapter we shall discuss it more fully. Plato left us an account of Atlantis, which met all the requirements necessary for the growth of a splendid culture earlier than any other: a civilization we could certainly regard as the cradle of all other ancient cultures.

Bearing Plato's story in mind, the island concerned might be one which has disappeared as a result of some natural calamity; but we must be ready to rediscover it with the modern techniques of research!

# Chapter Fourteen

Did Galanopoulos and Bacon create their own Atlantis?—
did Atlantis exist?—was Atlantis on the island of Santorini?

Plato (427–347 B.C.) left us two works which are relevant to the
story of Atlantis: his dialogues *Timaeus* and *Critias*. The first
of these deals with the creation of the universe and part of the
history of Atlantis, while the second describes Atlantis as Plato
heard about it. Solon is the key figure in the story and was
Plato's source of information. He was a very able statesman and
law-giver who gave Athens her constitution, together with some
democratic institutions such as the appointment of statesmen
by casting lots. The Romans also owed the fundamentals of their
own legislation to Solon. From many works it seems that he was
a meticulous man and dedicated to the truth, so there is no
reason at all to doubt the validity of the report Plato made on
the basis of what Solon had been told during a visit to the Egyptian city of Sais about 2,500 years ago.

A priest told Solon that the name of their goddess—Neith—
was the same as that of the Greek goddess Athena, and that
there was a relationship between the two races which was of the
greatest antiquity. When Solon explained to the priests what he
knew about the earliest history of the Greeks he was interrupted
by one of the older priests, and at this point we can let Plato
speak for himself:

"Solon, Solon, you Greeks are just children! There is no
such thing as an ancient Greek."

Solon thereupon inquired: "What do you mean by that?"

Whereupon the priest replied: "You are young in the spirit,
many though there may be of you. You have no ancient
beliefs based upon remote traditions, no body of know-

162

ledge, hoary with age. And the cause of this is that there were so many destructions of mankind in different ways; and it will be so in the future likewise. Fire and water wrought the greatest havoc, but thousands of others brought lesser disasters. You too know the legend of Phaeton, the son of Helios. On a certain day he yoked his father's chariot but being incapable of keeping to the correct path he burnt everything in the world and perished himself, struck by lightning.

"This seems like a myth when thus told; but its truth lies in the fact that the heavenly bodies moving around the world deviate from their courses and after a long time the earth is scorched and consumed in huge fires. At that moment the peoples of the mountains and high places will die before those near the rivers and the sea. The Nile floods and thus saves us from distress, as it has done so often before. But when the gods water the earth and flood it, the shepherds and cattle farmers in the mountains are safe, whereas your citizens are swept away into the sea. But here among us the water never flows down from above on to the ploughland; on the contrary, nature arranges that all the water wells up from the depths. That is why everything here is so old.

"There may well be some truth in this: in all the places where there is not too much cold or heat we find men, sometimes many, sometimes fewer.

"Now if among you yourselves or elsewhere anything great or lovely or strange occurs then one always finds that it has for a long time been inscribed here in our temples and safely kept. But with you and other peoples it is quite different. You have only just learnt to write and learn the things needed by a city and it is just at such a time that disasters befall you, such as disease. Only the unlettered and the primitive survive so that you have to start all over again like a new generation. You know nothing of what happened in ancient days at all and what you call history is nothing but a collection of fairy tales.

"For a start you know of only *one* Flood, but there were

many in the past. And furthermore you know nothing of the fact that the loveliest and most noble of all human races arose in your own land. You descend from them yourself and likewise your whole city, because a little of their seed survived.

"But you remained in ignorance of this because the survivors endured and died, generation after generation, without having ever learnt to express themselves in writing. Yes, Solon, there was once a time before the greatest of all inundations when the city of Athens shone out above all others in the war. She had the best laws and built the most beautiful buildings and possessed the finest government of all the nations."

Solon thereupon asked the priest to tell him the whole history. The priest agreed and explained: "Of the two states yours is the older, a thousand years older than ours. According to the sacred books the foundation of our state arose 8000 years ago. I will therefore tell you about your fellow-citizens living 9000 years ago."

The chapter that deals with Athene struggling with Atlantis is the most important section of the *Timaeus* for our purposes and it is worth giving a brief survey of it.

The priest relates how a great power which came from an alien part of the world in the Atlantic Ocean overwhelmed the whole of Europe and Asia. These invaders came from Atlantis, a group of islands *beyond* the Pillars of Hercules. The priest also describes how the men from the Atlantis islands reached the mainland on the far side of the "real ocean".

The attackers were fought to a standstill by the power of Athene, but both forces were exterminated by enormous earthquakes and floods, while the Atlantis islands were swallowed up by the sea; and that is how, the priest concludes, it comes about that the ocean in those parts is still inaccessible and cannot be explored because of all the mud lying just under the surface of the water.

\*    \*    \*

Having given an outline of the *Timaeus*, we would like to summarize the gist of Plato's *Critias*, in which we find another report about Atlantis, made perhaps by the same priest to Solon. Once again the priest states that Atlantis was *beyond* the Pillars of Hercules at Gibraltar, and that the story dates back about 9000 years. He gives Solon exact details of the capital city of the kingdom of Atlantis, where Atlas was king and where his brothers, amongst them Gadeirus, ruled over Gades.

The brothers were all sons of the god Poseidon (Neptune), who was pictured in the great temple of the city riding in a war-chariot drawn by six winged horses and accompanied by hundreds of sea-nymphs riding on the backs of dolphins.

The capital city apparently had an extensive canal system connecting it with the open sea, and inner harbours as well as covered and uncovered docks. The defence walls were built of three different sorts of stone which were coloured white, red and black. These were finished in yellow copper, tin and a metal called "orichalcum" which had a reddish glow, and was probably red copper.

The flat land around the city spread as far as 3000–2000 stadia (about 540–360 kilometres) and was very fertile as a result of the irrigation works. There were two harvests annually, part of which was exported! Flowers, fruit and varieties of grain grew wild, and many of them were cultivated.

The city possessed many parks and the fountains ran with warm and cool water from underground wells. Rain fell in the winter, and the excess was led off through aqueducts to reservoirs, some of which were covered over and used for bathing in the winter. The island in which the city lay was mountainous in the north and had many rivers, villages, lakes and pastures. There was also a hard kind of fruit which looked just like wood but provided drink, food and anointing-oil—which makes one think of coconuts!

There were also elephants on the island and large quantities of silver and gold which were used among other things for the decoration of the temples and the manufacture of statuary.

It is clearly stated in the *Critias* that the mainland which lay

165

around the "real ocean" could be reached from the Atlantis islands.

Plato ends his report by stating that the prosperity of Atlantis lasted for countless generations until in the end the people showed such decadence that the "father of the gods" wanted to punish them . . . it is in the middle of this sentence that Plato's account breaks off for reasons that have never yet been fathomed.

Over the centuries the accounts of Atlantis given in these two books have inspired thousands of publications dealing with the location of that lost kingdom. To judge by these works it seems that Atlantis might have been anywhere in the world; but although many of them put forward interesting arguments, Atlantis has never been found.

One theory is that Plato wanted to portray an ideal state and chose Atlantis for this purpose; yet if Plato had really wanted to do so he would never have gone to the such involved lengths about Solon, the priests, the early Greeks, and so on, nor would such a detailed description of the city and its environs have been necessary. Furthermore, the well-known fifth century A.D. philosophers Proclus and Syrianus carefully examined Plato's dialogues and fully supported them. The Greek Crantor also seems to have had complete faith in the dialogues, and he tells us that when he went on a visit to the Neith (Athene) temple in Sais he found some pillars covered in hieroglyphics which when translated were found to confirm Plato's dialogues in detail. There is no reason at all to believe in the ideal-state theory.

As we have said, throughout the centuries both experts and laymen have produced innumerable theories about the location of Atlantis, only a tiny fraction of which have had any scientific basis. The majority were only fit for amusing reading on a long winter evening, but two of them are worth mentioning. The German clergyman Jurgen Spanuth was convinced that Atlantis was situated near Heligoland, but unfortunately for him the experts decided that what he and a diver had found in the course of underwater research was not the ruins of Atlantis but natural geographical formations; and a Colonel Braghine believed that Atlantis vanished as a result of a collision between the earth and her "second moon", and that its remains are to be found in several islands in the Indian Ocean. Each theory speaks for itself; what is surprising is that both the authors' books were so widely read!

The sea between France and England has always been thought of as a possible site for Atlantis, but unhappily for those people who hold this theory the land has never actually sunk here: it was covered by water for reasons which can be adequately explained by science.

But the Atlantic Ocean remains the favourite, and every part of it has been regarded as a possible site for Atlantis. The Azores are a much favoured group of islands, yet it is often forgotten that the well-known American oceanographer, Eving, has demonstrated after extensive research that no large area of land has existed near these islands for the last twenty million years, at least none the size of Atlantis.

The bottom of the Atlantic is also ruled out, since several oceanographers have shown that the sea bed is far too thin and that there have been no basic changes in its structure since the evolution of mankind. Nor have any discoveries been made or drawings been found proving that a natural calamity took place.

The Atlantic ridge, which stretches over an enormous area, is another possibility, but quite apart from the fact that no geological changes have occurred since time immemorial, there are about 2000 metres of water covering its highest points, which does not square with Plato's account of mud just beneath the surface.

The most recent theory to be familiar to us was published for the first time in 1969 by Galanopoulos and Bacon in a book entitled *Atlantis, the Truth behind the Legend,* in which they claim that the volcanic island of Santorini in the Aegean is the original site of Atlantis. It is known from antiquity that this island was called Calliste (the "most beautiful"), and that it was also known as Thera.

A Swedish expedition to the island in 1947 showed that the

167

volcano on Thera had exploded in about 1400 B.C. with tremendous violence, with disastrous consequences not only for the island itself but also for surrounding areas. The explosion appears to have been far worse than Krakatoa in 1883; most of the island was blown away, and what remains is the present-day Santorini.

Clearly an eruption of such power would have had far-reaching consequences for nearby islands like Crete; and it is now known that about 1400 B.C. the Cretan state collapsed and hitherto flourishing communities were unsettled, if not wiped out.

The geological proof of this is unquestionable, and was therefore seized upon by Galanopoulos and Bacon in support of their theory; but we should add that they used numerous details supplied by the Swedish expedition and offered them as if they were their own. In their brilliantly illustrated book they maintain on the strength of geological evidence that Atlantis was where we now find Santorini, and to make their arguments acceptable they reject everything Plato has told us about Atlantis. They do not estimate Greek and Egyptian arithmetic skills very highly, nor do they agree with Plato's dimensions; and they also manage to discover new Pillars of Hercules.

As we have seen, Plato reckoned Atlantis had existed some 9000 years before his time, well before Solon's visit to Egypt. However, Galanopoulos and Bacon claim this resulted from a mistaken calculation by both the Greeks and the Egyptians, who had confused the sign for 100 for that for 1000, and as a result, the history of Atlantis is made to take place at a time much nearer to that of the volcanic explosion—and to Solon's visit to Egypt! In other words, they claim that Atlantis existed 900 years before Solon, rather than 9000! Yet the fact is that both the Greeks and the Egyptians had completely different signs for 100 and 1000!

We agree that Egyptian arithmetic was not very good, and this is something we discussed in our chapter dealing with Egypt; nor does it really matter very much if both the Egyptians *and* the Greeks were a century or two out in their dating of an event—but a mistake of 8000 years is going a bit far!

168

Plato gives the dimensions of the area as 3000 stadia by 2000—540 by 360 kilometres. Thera, the original Atlantis according to Galanopoulos and Bacon, was not anything like this size! So presumably comparable mistakes must have been made in the calculations here as well, in which case the figures given for the surface area would have to be reduced to 54 by 36 kilometres, which is rather closer to the original size of Thera

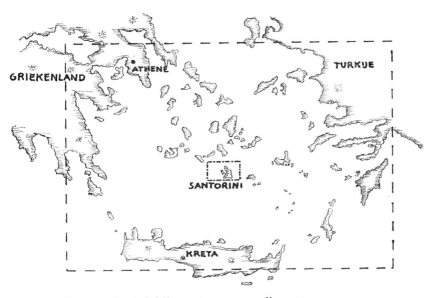

Fig. 31.   54 by 36 kilometres according to Galanopoulos and Bacon. But Plato's Atlantis is 540 by 360 kilometres!

(fig. 31)! The obvious solution to the problem of how to reconcile Plato's account with our own theories is to rely on supposed mathematical errors!

There is more to come! The siting of Atlantis in the Aegean Sea does not square with what Plato tells us. Plato, Solon and the Egyptians all knew very well that the Mediterranean was an inland sea, and they were well aware of the existence of the Atlantic Ocean! This was why Plato stated that Atlantis was *beyond* the Pillars of Hercules, and that from it men could reach the mainland "encircling the true ocean"!

Because Gibraltar as the Pillars of Hercules did not fit in with their theory, Galanopoulos and Bacon were obliged to look for new Pillars, which they found in the capes of Matapan and Maleas, the southernmost fork of the Peloponnese; yet they overlooked the fact that at no time in the ancient world had these capes ever been referred to as the Pillars of Hercules, whereas Gibraltar was often identified with them.

Furthermore, these gentlemen interpret the other "similarities" between Atlantis and Santorini in a very liberal way. For instance, they often refer to the three types of stone which Plato had mentioned and point out, as if it mattered, that the red, white and black colours of the different types of stone are also found on the island of Santorini—which seems reasonable enough when one remembers that one can find stones of these colours on nearly every volcanic island (and there are a good many of them)! Then they deal with the sulphurous wells, which again are common on volcanic islands; and a great deal is made of the fruitfulness of the Santorini soil—which is nothing special either—and the ruins of buildings and irrigation works. They refer to Plato at this point, without realizing that these were not the work of the people of Atlantis but of the Phoenicians, who were firmly established on the island long before the fatal explosion. We have an account of this by Herodotus, and it seems likely that his version, together with the Swedish findings, played a *very* large part in the development of this theory!

Herodotus was an important historian of the fifth century B.C. who tells us that Calliste was inhabited in earlier times by the Phoenicians, who fished there for the murex mollusc—a purple dye is produced from one of its glands, which Phoenicians used in manufacturing their famous Tyrian purple. Cadmus was supposed to have brought these traders to the island, and to have introduced the art of writing to Greece; and archaeologists have in fact found the earliest Greek alphabets there, an alphabet which had not yet developed double consonants.

Much later, in the twelfth century B.C.—and thus after the

170

eruption—the Lacedaemonians arrived under the leadership of Theras, whose name was given to the island, replacing Calliste.

Unfortunately Herodotus did not supply any dates; however he certainly never mentions the possibility of Thera's history going still farther back or of there having been another civilization there.

He does however describe the nearby island of Samos, which could boast of an even earlier history, and which he felt contained all kinds of wonders. Among those he mentions was an aqueduct that ran underground through the base of a hill at one stage for about one and a half kilometres; what made it especially noteworthy, according to Herodotus, was the fact that its builders began to tunnel from both sides of the hill at once, and when they met they were hardly a metre out in their calculations!

Herodotus also describes the construction of the so-called "Polycrates aqueduct", which he attributes to the architect Eupalinus of Mega. The island had a flourishing culture and he was full of admiration for the capital city which lay near a large, flat expanse of land, was rich in buildings, temples and parks and got its water supply from an aqueduct. There was also a specially constructed harbour with a dam 400 metres long and "twenty fathoms deep"; he considered the temple of Hera to be the greatest in Greece at the time.

Samos is further described as an extremely prosperous island and other details are sufficient for us to see that it has striking similarities with Plato's portrayal of Atlantis. But Samos was not good enough for Galanopoulos and Bacon when compared, for instance, with their speculations about Matapan and Maleas; nor could they change the time of the actual disaster in order to be able to explain the destruction of Atlantis.

Yet certain ideas are suggested by the account given by Herodotus, by the work of the Swedish expedition, and by the idea that Atlantis may be Santorini, not least because the whole theory would seem to suggest that Plato was wrong in nearly every respect! If one examines the Galanopoulos and Bacon theory closely one quite clearly realizes that they are dealing with a different Atlantis which has nothing in common with that of Plato. Now that we have discussed both this theory and Plato's writings on the subject, let us have a look at Santorini itself for a moment.

It is believed that the first Stone Age farmers settled in the Aegean about 9000 years ago, and it was not until approximately 3000 B.C. that one could speak of an early Bronze Age in the region according to carbon 14 datings. The latter date is disputed, but 3000 B.C. seems to be on the safe side—which would mean that several thousand years lie between that time and the date of Atlantis provided by Plato! Plato's dialogues make it clear that for thousands of years before this the people of Atlantis had used a great variety of metals, which is not easy to square with the theory that Atlantis was on Santorini.

Furthermore it is known that all civilizations influence "parallel cultures" elsewhere, and that people have always traded and exchanged presents; and since these goods were put into the burial-chambers one can ascertain fairly accurately who had contact with whom. For instance, cylinder seals from the Indus have been found in Sumerian graves, and seals from the Land of Two Rivers in Egyptian ones. There are many examples of this sort of thing—but why have no traces of Atlantis ever been found on the island of Santorini? Or indeed anywhere in the Aegean?

Plato says that the Atlantis race had a highly developed culture and engaged in a good deal of trade and exporting so some artefacts should at least have been discovered in the Aegean originating in a culture that was both alien to us and much older than any we now know; yet so far nothing of this kind has ever been found. All the discoveries that have been made show Cretan, Egyptian or Trojan influence or derivation, and none of them are nearly old enough to have originated in Atlantis. Naturally bones, potsherds and other objects have been discovered, but they all belong without exception to the original inhabitants of these regions and definitely not to an advanced culture of the order of Atlantis.

This particular problem could, however, be solved. Even if

survivors from Atlantis—or the Ancients—had come here without being able to bring much with them after the disaster(s), they might still have left a strong cultural influence; but this is certainly not the case.

If Atlantis really was Santorini, then Plato was writing a fairy story (and a very inaccurate one at that), while Solon, Proclus, Syrianus and many others were either mistaken or were indulging in an early form of science fiction: this might be true of one individual but not of people who were otherwise famous for their extreme integrity.

But just suppose Atlantis was in fact on Santorini. It would then have been one of a large group of cultures that existed around 3000 B.C. in the Mediterranean area. We know a great deal about Egypt, Crete, Mesopotamia, Troy and other areas at that time and we would have to assume that Atlantis had a similar level of cultural achievement; yet this quite contradicts Plato. Like you, we prefer to believe these trusty messengers from the distant past rather than all the publications about Atlantis which have appeared through the centuries and will continue to do so!

We are convinced that Atlantis existed, but we do not claim to know where. Many readers will see this as a contradiction in terms, since we claim to believe in Atlantis while rejecting a number of theories after examining them critically.

One thing is certain: we can accept no theory which puts Atlantis in the Atlantic Ocean near Gibraltar. We have a great deal of faith in what Plato said, and in Chapter Thirteen we discussed in detail the advantages a large, fertile island would have held for the growth of human civilization there; yet how can we reconcile belief in the existence of Atlantis, with a denial that it could ever have been in the Atlantic as we know it today?

In the first place, those who believe this are making a serious error of judgement. The Atlantic Ocean meant something very different to the ancient Greeks and Egyptians than it does to us: they called the ocean beyond the Pillars of Hercules the Atlantic without ever realizing its size or making any attempt to find out what its limits were. Any area outside the Mediterranean was the "Atlantic"; including the Indian and Pacific oceans! Atlantis could have been anywhere! Every ship that sailed in through the Pillars of Hercules came from the "Atlantic", even if its port of origin had been, as it were, in Japan! The same applied to Atlantis, which, in theory at least, might have been in the Indian Ocean! We have already shown you that it was very unlikely to have been in the Atlantic, and we hope that future investigators will not make the same mistake as their predecessors over the centuries—mistakes which drove them to search for Atlantis in places where there was nothing to find!

No doubt this problem will be solved in the future; and to find the answer we must try to find the real Ancients who, we believe, possessed a culture which has not yet come to light. But in doing so let us restrict ourselves to our own planet and leave the "extra-terrestrial civilizations" in peace; after all, they will find things difficult enough in the future, whenever man starts to bother himself about them!

Finally, it is worth remembering that the American oceanographer Bruce Heeze has claimed that when the last Ice Age ended, the sea level in some areas rose quite considerably, sometimes by more than a hundred metres. This would have occurred 11,000 years ago—or bearing Plato's version of Atlantis in mind, perhaps 9000 years before Solon's visit to Egypt?

# PART FOUR

# The Discovery of America

# Chapter Fifteen

The swastika, one of the oldest and most enigmatic signs known to man.

Despite its extremely unpleasant associations, the swastika or, if you prefer, the hooked cross, is one of our oldest symbols. It can be found throughout the Indo-European countries and far beyond them as well. Some people even see in it a remnant of Atlantis.

Its great antiquity has been demonstrated by the archaeologist Carl William Blegen, who is well-known as a result of his excavations in Troy. In Troy Four he unearthed a cylindrical lid dating from about 2050–1900 B.C. which had a swastika on it, as well as other signs. It is not clear what value the Trojans attached to the sign but undoubtedly it had some symbolic meaning.

The swastika has been found in many other places, including the ancient culture of the Indus; it is also mentioned in the Ramayana, and frequently occurs on old stone temples in India. It occurs in China as one of the 108 signs on the Buddha's feet; it was also a symbol of the Buddha's heart. If the Glozel signs are authentic, and the archaeologist Salmon Reinach's datings are correct, then the swastika was known there too, since it has been found on clay tablets about 6000 years old! The Glozel finds have been discussed by us elsewhere, so it is sufficient to say that the symbol seems to have been part of the Glozel alphabet. In this respect its use is rather different from its symbolic significance elsewhere.

What significance should we attach to the swastika? We do not know for certain, but it seems increasingly likely that it was a symbol of the sun, and this is suggested by the similarity of many other symbols to the form of the swastika.

But its symbolic meaning is not so important here: what is more interesting and of more consequence is the fact that the sign occurs on the so-called "mounds" of North America, in the Central American civilizations and on a small island near the Haiti coast in the Caribbean. On this little island, Ile à Vache, the archaeologist Godfrey J. Olsen found a stone sphere with several swastikas inscribed upon it (fig. 32)! It is estimated to be about 2000 years old — maybe not as ancient as the Trojan one, but still fascinating!

Fig. 32. Stone basin with swastikas. Found on the island, Ile à Vache, near Haiti.

As far as the old cultures of Europe, Asia, India and China are concerned, it seems probable that the use of the swastika slowly spread outwards from a central point of origin to cover an enormous area, since contact overland between these regions was possible. This does not hold true for North America, Central America and the Ile à Vache, isolated as they are by the oceans, in spite of which thousands of swastikas have been found; so naturally we want to know how they came to be there.

Chance is ruled out. It is not unlikely that races with no contact between them might share elementary designs like the circle and the cross, since nothing is simpler than to draw two intersecting lines or a circle. But the swastika is different; with the four extensions to the arms of the cross, it is much more complicated. It would have been more logical to have come across a form of swastika in one or other of these isolated cultures in which the extensions were not at the ends of the arms but half-way down them: but no such signs have been discovered, and we are left with the problem of how the swastika managed to appear on the other side of the ocean. If we play for safety and take as an example the most recent of the swastikas found in America, namely those of the Ile à Vache, we must still ask which ancient seafaring nation was capable of crossing the ocean at the time of Christ's birth.

Frankly, we do not know. And yet the number of finds proving that America was discovered long before Columbus is steadily growing. We also know that the mound-builders of North America had no contact with the civilizations of Central America—at least there is absolutely no proof that they did. Yet the swastika is found in both areas, so we must assume that this is not a matter of an isolated and accidental discovery of America, but of some great seafaring race having paid several visits to North and Central America. It is unlikely that a single, isolated visit would have persuaded the local inhabitants to adopt the swastika as a motif for burial-chamber decoration; they would not have used an alien sign for their graves and their implements.

So we must ask ourselves this: was the swastika brought to the New World by the Ancients?

# Chapter Sixteen

Did Columbus know where he could find America?

We think he did: an experienced sailor, who had been inspired by a book and possibly supplied with a marine chart, sailed to America—and that is exactly what Columbus was!

Christopher Columbus (Cristóbal Colón) was born at Genoa in 1451. He was not of noble birth, contrary to what the history books often tell us. He was the son of a weaver, who also owned a shop selling liquor. He learnt the art of weaving wool from his father, but although he mastered the basic elements of reading, writing and arithmetic he never went to a university such as the one at Pavia. His Latin has sometimes been praised, but it was in fact a kind of dog-Latin, the "Latin genovisco". But it is true that he was exceptionally keen to learn, and that he devoured book after book; he was a typical self-taught person, and not the scholastic prodigy some authors would have us believe. In 1479 he settled in Lisbon where, in about 1480, he married Doña Felipa Moñiz Perestrello, the daughter of an old and aristocratic seafaring family; and it was through this marriage that Columbus was introduced to the Portuguese court.

On the death of his father-in-law he inherited some nautical instruments, maps, notes and other material concerning sea voyages; and it was at this time that he probably began a friendship with the German mathematician and cartographer, Martin Behain, who lived in Lisbon from 1484 to 1490 and was later given a Portuguese knighthood by King John the Second of Portugal.

We know that Columbus made a number of journeys to England and to Guinea, and in the document referring to the journey to England we find an odd passage: "I sailed one hundred miles on the other side of the island of Tile (Thule). It was to this island, which is as big as England, that Englishmen came with their goods, mostly from Bristol."

It has often been maintained that the island "as big as England" that Columbus visited was Iceland; experts have remarked on the Norse colonies in Greenland, Estribygo and Vestribyo, with "Markland and Weinland" to the south, and consider it possible that Columbus might have had access to maps showing such areas—perhaps a portolan, or a map by Donnus Nikolaus Germanus, or even the controversial Vinland map which appears to date from 1440 and upon which Isolanda (Iceland), Gronelanda (Greenland) and Vinlanda (Vinland) are shown. But apart from the considerable nautical discrepancies involved in this interpretation, Columbus himself says in his log-book entry for December 21st when reporting the first journey in 1492 that the northernmost land he visited was England and the most southerly was Guinea; all of which are good reasons for treating claims that he visited Iceland with some misgivings.

Yet it is possible that he may have had access to maps like that of Donnus Nikolaus Germanus—also known as Dominus Nicolaus Germanus—or even those of the Danish cartographer, Claudius Clausson, several copies of whose maps were scattered throughout Europe. From the knowledge that there was land to the north-west of the Atlantic it was only one step to the hypothesis that there must also be land at a lower latitude on the other side of the Atlantic.

Around 1474 the Portuguese king requested Toscanelli, a cosmographer living in Florence, to send him information about the shortest way to India. Toscanelli's reply dated June 25th 1474, is still extant and in it he says that the quickest route was westwards over the Atlantic Ocean. His letter was accompanied by a signed map. Columbus had somehow got to hear about this exchange of letters, and having at once contacted Toscanelli he received a copy of the same map, together with a letter, in which Toscanelli also discusses in detail the strange things to be seen in India. He actually wrote as follows:

"Learn likewise that on all these islands merchants live and trade: there are large numbers of ships, goods, sailors and merchants. The land is very heavily populated; it has many provinces and kingdoms and numberless cities under the leadership of a prince called the Great Khan.

"This land is more worth visiting than others. One can not only make great gains there and obtain many things but there are also gold, silver, gems and large quantities of spices of all imaginable kinds such as we never see. It is fitting that white men of letters, wise men, astrologers and other excellent scholars familiar with all the arts should rule that splendid land and fight battles there. Florence. Toscanelli."

There is also a later letter from him to Columbus giving details of the distances to India.

Yet nine years were to elapse after this correspondence before Columbus placed his ideas before the Portuguese king, and in the end the Portuguese court rejected his plan to sail westwards in order to find India. Their refusal, however, was undoubtedly prompted by the completely unacceptable demands made by Columbus. It seems very likely that Columbus knew exactly where he wanted to go but wished to conceal his intentions from the Portuguese, and later the Spaniards, by pretending that he was hoping to find the shorter route to India instead.

Among his demands were ten per cent of all profits earned by this and *all* future voyages; elevation to the aristocracy; nomination as viceroy and governor of any lands found by him for the duration of his life, these titles to be handed on to his firstborn child; and a say in the appointment of government officials and in all commercial and economic measures taken.

These demands hardly seem to tally with conditions in India, which at that time was excellently organized under an outstandingly good government. Certainly India had no need of foreign intervention, nor did the Portuguese then have the means of subjecting India to their rule. In addition to the other conditions imposed, Columbus wanted Portugal to finance the whole enterprise; he never withdrew his demands, even when he submitted his plan to the Spanish royal family in 1490, who similarly rejected it.

Columbus returned to Portugal after this, but at once made fresh attempts to gain another audience with the Spaniards—which was actually achieved the following year. This time his project was accepted in spite of his exorbitant demands, as a result of which it became known as the Treaty of Capitulation.

Did Columbus have fresh evidence? It seems very probable, otherwise there would have been no reason for the Spaniards accepting his proposals and placing ships at the disposal of an "outsider", let alone financing the whole undertaking and yielding to his exorbitant demands!

Finding a shorter route to India had little to do with the Capitulation Treaty as far as Columbus was concerned. We must remember that in 1497 Bartholomew Dias sailed round the Cape of Good Hope, thus opening up the eastern route to India, with the result that King John of Portugal had no further interest in any westerly route. The triumphal entry of Bartholemew Dias into Lisbon harbour was closely observed by Columbus.

Columbus' plan to sail across the Atlantic must have taken shape quite early in view of his correspondence with Toscanelli and his familiarity with the book *Imago Mundi*, to which we shall refer later. Columbus also describes how during his visit to Porto Santo, an island near Madeira, he saw unusually large clumps of a peculiar kind of reed lapping against the shore, along with a strangely shaped piece of wood. He learnt that at Flores in the Azores the bodies of two men had been washed up which had "quite different facial and bodily features"; and he knew furthermore of small craft that were constructed from a single tree-trunk, since pieces of pinewood of an unknown sort were often washed up. All this, together with the statements made by various sea-captains and pilots at Palos—from whence he would depart for America—supports the notion that Columbus must have known that there was land to the west. There is also an account of a Portuguese captain who discovered an island when sailing west of the Azores; he took away some sand from the beach to use in his stove, and later some grains of gold were found in it (this story has not been checked by us).

Once Columbus had become quite firmly convinced that land existed to the west, he faced the problem of convincing others to form an expedition with him. He would never have succeeded if he had suggested that there was an unknown land on the other side of the ocean, since the idea would not have appealed in the slightest to those who were going to finance the expedition. There is a great deal to support the theory that Columbus emphasized the theory that there was a shorter way to India, which could certainly be found and would lead to the discovery of great kingdoms for the picking! He based his proposition on the spherical nature of the world. By exploiting human greed in this way, he saw that it would be much easier to convince the princes of the realm of the practicality of such an expedition to "India", and to justify his very considerable heavy demands on them. This would also explain why Columbus had to insist later on that he had found "India", as we can see from his log book, which he knew in advance would get into the hands of the Spanish rulers. On no account could Columbus have admitted that, on the pretext of sailing to India, he had managed to talk the Spanish monarchy into giving him three ships, together with all the necessary money and equipment, while being at the same time quite certain in his own mind that he would not be looking for India. He must have realized shortly after his discovery of America that it was not India; he was too intelligent and too good a navigator for that!

It is a pity that only small sections of his log book are still extant—in the Alva family archives in Madrid—and that in order to study the documents one must refer to the copy made by the bishop, Bartolemeo de las Casas, the *Historia de las Indias*, even though it does appear to be fairly reliable.

The time has now come for Columbus to depart and, on August 3rd 1492 three ships, excellently equipped, left Palos harbour in the direction of the Canaries. It is still not known why Columbus sailed a thousand miles to the south before heading west, since he had already decided to make for the Canary Islands before the rudder of the caravel *Pinta* ceased to function

184

properly on August 6th. In any case the main part of the voyage began on September 6th from Gomera harbour.

Almost as soon as the journey had begun, Columbus hid from his crew details of the actual number of miles logged each day. He always announced fewer than had actually been covered in order to prevent the men from grumbling about the length of the return journey: but did he then realize how many miles would have to be covered before any mainland would be reached? By October 1st 2828 miles had been covered—but the crew were given a figure of 2336 miles!

An interesting entry in this log book occurs on Tuesday, September 25th, when Columbus requested Martin Alonso Pinzón, skipper of the *Pinta*, to hand him a chart which he had lent him three days previously which showed the presence of islands in that part of the ocean. What map could this have been and who had prepared it? And what islands did it refer to? Columbus had by this time already completed more than two-thirds of his voyage, and as yet we know nothing certain about sea-journeys across the Atlantic undertaken before his own; if the map had been correct somebody must have come across islands in this area, but the islands shown on the map were never found in spite of course variations.

On October 12th—seventy days after leaving Palos—they sighted land at last, an island which Columbus called San Salvador. Contact was made with the natives and here Columbus at once started to make inquiries about gold, which was used by the local people as a decoration for their pierced nostrils. Columbus was told to sail further south where he would find it in large quantities; the voyage continued, and landings were made at Cuba and Haiti, but he was forced to sail for home because of the shipwreck of the *Santa Maria* and the independent actions of the *Pinta*. However, Columbus made sure he took with him as evidence of his voyage six American Indians complete with gold masks and a number of other objects, also largely of gold.

One point deserves special attention: according to Columbus' own story they had taken with them from Spain considerable quantities of glass beads and marbles as well as copper bells to exchange for gold. But—and this point is usually overlooked—is it likely that they would have taken such things with them if they were going to India, itself so rich and highly developed? The Indians would have greeted them with scorn! And we must remember that Columbus knew very well what India was like. Toscanelli had written to say that it was rich in gold, silver, precious stones and exotic spices of all kinds; he also highly praised its buildings, its royal edifices, its two hundred cities, the skills of its craftsmen and, in general, the high level of civilization found there. Columbus also had access to other sources of information about India, so can we really believe that he would have attempted to exchange glass marbles for Indian gold? Certainly not! Columbus was after undiscovered country, and he must have had a fairly good idea where he could find it!

We referred earlier to his close friendship with the German cartographer, Martin Behain, and it was in Germany that we came across a particularly curious map in the course of our researches. It was contained in an early book, dated 1482 but brought up to date in 1510 by a certain Glareanus, whom we shall refer to in the next chapter: the book is called the *Ptolemaeus Cosmographia*, and is supplied with a Latin text by Jac. Angelo. This so-called Glareanus map has a Ptolemaic projection of the type in use up to the Middle Ages (plate 27), and its most curious feature is that Greenland and the Americas are clearly shown, with a projection involving both eastern and western coastlines. The extended South American outline is very clearly outlined, together with details first provided by Columbus after his first journey; and South America is not joined to the South Pole, but ends in a point—a feature of South American geography that only became clear in maps of a much later period! Remember that South America was not circumnavigated by Fernando de Magellan until 1521–2—and even then he did not sail back up the west coast but headed straight out into the Pacific after rounding the Horn!

How old was the information on which this map was based. The only logical conclusion one can come to is that long before the time of Columbus, before he or Magellan were even born, voyages of discovery had been made along the coasts of the Americas—along both the eastern *and* the western shores! We do not yet know who undertook these voyages, but one thing is certain: America is so clearly demarcated on this map that nobody can merely attribute it to chance.

There is also the evidence of the Turkish admiral Piri Reis, a compiler of just such enigmatic charts (plates 25 and 26), or rather the remnants of them: it is a pity they are not complete, but are torn-off sections of larger maps. The maps date from 1513, and present numerous problems; for instance, they show the eastern seaboard of Central, North and South America, though the latter appears to join up with the South Pole, and is therefore not so accurately drawn as in the Glareanus map.

We must be careful about relying on these Piri Reis charts since it is quite possible that only a limited part of the northeast coast of South America is in fact depicted, and not the whole eastern seaboard! All we can say with certainty is that a section of South America is shown; the "mythical" additions, the degrees of latitude and longitude, the two compasses and the distance scales seem to suggest that only a limited area is covered —but, once again, this needs to be thoroughly investigated before we can come to a decision!

Even Greenland is shown on the second of these maps (plate 26), and although various writers have written about the subject they appear to have been unaware of the existence of this second Piri Reis map!

The amount of information contained in the Piri Reis and Glareanus maps must have resulted from decades—if not centuries—of research; and one must not forget that the information shown on these maps cannot have been collected together in the years following Columbus' "discovery" of America. They were in all probability the work of sailors who had made the journeys over decades, if not centuries, as well as of those who compiled the maps! Once again we must re-write our history, certainly as far as Columbus and Magellan are concerned!

The same Turkish admiral, Piri Reis, also wrote the *Kitab i Bahriye* which he prepared as a handbook for sailors. This work

187

was not only important for navigation in the Mediterranean at the time of the Ottoman Empire, but also contained a vast amount of other information; and to our amazement we find that Columbus is mentioned here too!

Piri Reis writes about the "westerly sea"—an early name for the Atlantic—and states that there is land on the far side, which had been navigated by the "incredulous" Genoa sailor, Columbus. Note that he says "navigated", not "discovered"! He maintains that Columbus was inspired by a book containing information about these lands, which were claimed to be rich in all sorts of metals and strange gems.

Piri Reis also says that: "This man Columbus tried with the book in his hand to convince the Portuguese and Genoese that an expedition would be very worthwhile. His ideas were rejected and so he turned to the Spanish bey (overlord). Here too his first request was not granted, but was later on accepeted after the matter had been pressed."

Judging by his reports and maps, Piri Reis appears to have been a reliable and meticulous man; and he emphasizes that all his statements rely on factual evidence, including those he makes about Columbus.

What was the book that gave Columbus the inspiration to cross the Atlantic? He himself gives us the answer: he tells us that it was the *Imago Mundi*, by the French cardinal, Pierre d'Ailly (also known as Aliaco, or Petrus Alliacus), a philosopher, astrologist and cosmographer at the University of Paris. It is known that he had put forward the suggestion that there was land beyond the Atlantic, which he based on his belief that the world was round.

Columbus was anyway an enterprising sailor; inspired by the *Imago Mundi* and equipped with his map and all the other necessary proofs, he was able to convince the Spanish leaders of the usefulness of an expedition to "India"/America. It may be that during his last, successful attempt to persuade them he had yet more evidence at his disposal, since he still insisted on his conditions, and which must have caused him a great deal of trouble. Yet Columbus deserves a special place in history, for his achievement has yielded pride of place only to that of the original discoverers of America, whoever they were. Columbus was a great sailor—but he was not the discoverer of America!

Elsewhere in this book, when writing about the Ancients, we point out that their sailors were by no means confined to the Mediterranean and that it may even have been the Phoenicians or the Carthaginians who first reached America. Numerous finds, which are increasing in number, seem to confirm this theory, but it is still fiercely contested. Yet it is in no way impossible because, as we have seen in the case of Columbus and Magellan, new discoveries can put supposedly "hard facts" in a completely different light. What is certain is that the Vikings at least reached North America before the time of Columbus, and their ships were not superior to those of the ancient races of the Mediterranean who lived long before our own era!

Furthermore we cannot believe that such peoples would have remained at home rather than explore the distant and undiscovered regions of the world. This would have been contrary to one of mankind's most basic attributes!

# Chapter Seventeen

The cartographical proof that America was discovered before the time of Columbus!—the oldest and most complete map of America!—a German geographical infant prodigy —Waldseemüller's map was not the first!

Many writers inspired by the "cosmic" theme have paid close attention to the Piri Reis map, and some of them have talked in terms of "maps", when in fact they were discussing a single chart. However, as we have seen, there actually is a second map (plate 26), which is unknown to any of these authors; and there are several dozen depicted in the already-mentioned *Kitab i Bahriye*, which was a sort of ancient nautical handbook that ran into several editions. However, the maps in the book cover the Mediterranean and occasionally the British Isles, whereas the other two deal mainly with America.

We will not discuss here the fantastic stories told about these maps, although it is amusing to compare them and to see how they fail to agree with each other in the slightest detail, even about the origin and the location of the maps. Our photographs were taken from the originals in the Topkapi Sarayi Museum at Istanbul; we propose to take a closer look at these charts and say why, in spite of all the nonsense written about them, they deserve the closest scrutiny.

The Piri Reis maps are, in fact, only fragments of larger ones. One can clearly see the torn edges, and what might appear to be the west coast of South America on the map shown in plate 25 is simply where the bend in the map occurs (it is untorn on this side)—yet many people have assumed it to be an outline of the west coast of South America. In fact the map only deals with the east coast, and probably only a part of that.

Piri Reis, whose place and time of birth are unknown, contrary to the opinions of some writers, spent his whole life in the service of the sea. As a youngster he must have accompanied his famous uncle, Kemal Reis, on countless sea voyages: they lived at Gallipolis, to which numerous Christian ships were brought. Piri Reis tells us how, as a result, he came into possession of a large quantity of marine maps, nautical instruments, and so forth, which he obtained by force or otherwise from the crews of these vessels.

The famous Piri Reis chart was drawn at Gallipolis in 1513, as a note on the map itself tells us. Like its companion, it is a typical example of the so-called "portolano", although this was the first and perhaps the only one to cover America. The portolano was initially created for use mainly in the Mediterranean, and was an Italian discovery originating in the ports of Genoa and Pisa; the oldest known example is the Carta Pisana, which probably dates from the end of the thirteenth century. One of their characteristics is that they only give details of coast-lines, ports, harbours, estuaries and landmarks: the hinterland was of no interest to the map-makers since the charts were meant solely for short sea voyages and coast voyages. Degrees of latitude and longitude were not usually shown—this was a practice that did not develop until the sixteenth century—but they did carry compasses and loxodromes, intersecting lines drawn from a compass by means of which a course could be charted.

The Reis charts belong to the portolan type in every respect. On a typical portolan harbours would be shown in various colours, so that a sailor could see at a glance what facilities the port possessed; black was used to indicate virtually unknown ports and red for the better-known ones—exactly as in the Piri Reis maps. Shallows and obstacles were marked by dots and crosses, which are only just visible to the reader on the Reis charts.

It also seems that the ships that have been drawn on the maps do not have a merely decorative function, any more than they do on other portolans, but are supposed to indicate wind

191

directions and currents. Doldrum areas are indicated by a picture of a ship with its sails struck.

Strikingly enough, the Piri Reis maps appear to be the only Turkish contribution to the development of the portolan; but in this one must of course include the mapping of the American east coast, which was done with a degree of exactitude hardly feasible so soon after Columbus' journeys. Even more striking is the fact that the Reis maps should both yield more information than the four Columbus voyages and cover a much wider area.

Piri Reis—who perished miserably, alas!—was appointed commander of the Egyptian fleet, Egypt having been a part of the Ottoman Empire since 1517, which meant that he did not stay in his familiar Mediterranean, but was based in the Red Sea and its environs. The Ottomans did not much care for the open sea at this time, and suffered grievously at the hands of the Portuguese who were supreme in this part of the world. Piri Reis does not seem to have fared too well because he returned to Suez in 1551, with the battered remnants of his ships; and his failure in the Red Sea must account for his committal for trial in 1552 or 1553. Happily he left us his *Kitab i Bahriye* and the maps—a fascinating inheritance from an exceedingly skilled seaman.

We must clarify one matter: these maps may be questionable and none too reliable, but it is nonsense to suppose, as some "cosmidiots" do, that they were made by aerial photography. Surely it is perfectly clear that they are marine charts, intended solely for shipping and nothing else! Some critics complain that the hinterland is not shown clearly enough, but—as we have seen—that is typical of the portolan! Some question whether or not Greenland and the South Pole are shown, while other experts are at loggerheads about further points of disagreement. But the essential point is that these maps give us details of the east coast of South America and other areas *before* Magellan went on his voyage!

We should mention that many early charts, which are still much more recent than those of Piri Reis, show South America ending in the South Pole rather than in a tip with a navigable channel to the south of it, as is actually the case.

There are three alternatives put forward to explain the Reis maps: firstly, that the whole east coast is in fact shown to be contiguous with the South Pole and Antarctica; secondly, that the area shown is merely a section of the north-eastern parts of South America; and thirdly, that practically the whole of the east coast is shown, but not as far south as Cape Horn, since nothing is indicated of the Straits of Magellan.

Having studied the map in some detail, we are inclined to accept the second suggestion, namely that the map gives only a limited portion of north-eastern South America. It seems unlikely that the whole of South America is portrayed; however we have not yet had sufficient time in which to study the evidence.

A great deal of interest has been aroused by the map made by Martin Waldseemüller of Radolfzell in 1507 which not only proclaimed America for the first time, but was also supposed to have outlined the east and west coasts of South America in precise detail (fig. 33).

We have discovered—as far as we were able to decipher it— a number of Portuguese names appear in this map, including Montpasqual, Rio de Brasil, Rio de S. Anthomo and, near the bottom of the map, Rio Iordan, followed lastly by Rio de Cananor. We then compared this map with another by Waldseemüller, the *Tabula Terre Nove*, Ptolemaeus Geographia, Strasburg 1513 (fig. 34). This gives us degrees of latitude, together with the same series of Portuguese place-names, with Rio de Cananor likewise at the bottom, clearly positioned around the 35 degrees latitude. Since Waldseemüller has clearly shown the equator on this map, as well as the "Tropicus Capricorn", even the layman can see that Rio de Cananor must have been to the north of present day Rio de la Plata—which means that on both maps an enormous area of South America is missing!

What some people see as the west coast of South America on the left of the 1507 Waldseemüller chart is no more than a map decoration, which is elsewhere quite clearly recognizable as such; and neither the 1507 nor the 1513 maps show the whole of South

Fig. 33. Martin Waldseemüller's map dating from 1507 on which the name "America" appears for the first time and which led to the belief that it showed both the east and west coasts.

America. Here again, Waldseemüller has simply reproduced part of the north-eastern section of South America, and nothing more!

Having looked at the Piri Reis and Waldseemüller maps we can now turn to the Glareanus charts. During our researches we came across a 1482 incunabulum (wood-print) issued by Leonardus Holl in Ulm with a translation by J. Angelo. It forms part

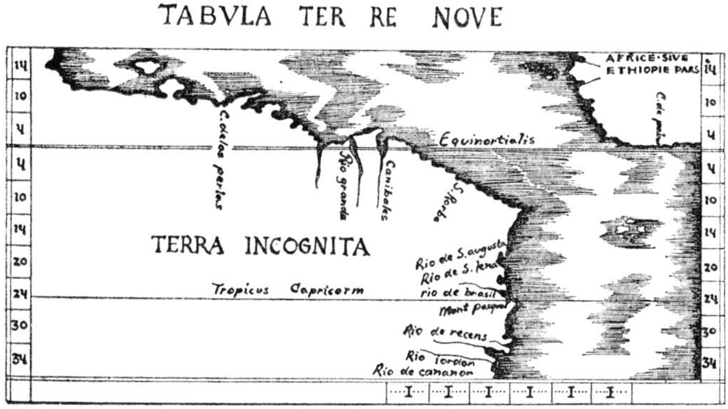

TABVLA TER RE NOVE

Fig. 34. Martin Waldseemüller's map dating from 1513.

of an early book, *Ptolemaeus Geographia*, which is in the written manuscript section of the Bonn University Library in the Adenauerallee.

As we have seen, the Martin Waldseemüller maps of 1507 and 1513 both show the north-east region of South America, while the Piri Reis map again shows the east coast, possibly running into Antarctica, or at any rate revealing a larger area than those of Waldseemüller: there were still seven years to go before Magellan began his voyage, which presents something of a problem!

But the map we came across, the so-called Glareanus map (plate 27) not only quite clearly shows the whole of South America, including both the east *and* the west coast, but also the southernmost tip of the continent, definitely indicating that it has been circumnavigated! Part of the Caribbean region is also outlined on this global map, together with sections of North

195

America which it has always been thought, were still undiscovered in 1510! The first person to open up these areas was the adventurer Vasco Nunes Balboa, who actually crossed the Panama Isthmus in 1510 itself! The evidence is piling up!

However, there is a great deal more to be said about the Glareanus chart. The Latin heading at the top—which is visible to the reader, though not legible—tells us that the work on the map was completed in 1510 by the Swiss scholar Heinrich Loris (Glareanus), otherwise known as Henricus Loris or Loreti or Henricus Loretide Glaris, who was born on April 3rd 1488.

One can clearly see from the text that Glareanus improved and completed the original map, which was based on data known since the time of Claudius Ptolemaeus, the second century Alexandrian astronomer. Ptolemy originated the use of lines of latitude and longitude—by which he charted 8000 place-names—and his work in cartography was influential right up until the sixteenth century!

The Glareanus text on the map runs as follows:

"Although, dear reader, nobody doubts that the eminent geographers of ancient times were very zealous in this respect we must openly admit that much knowledge was withheld from them. This is quite clear from the eight books of Ptolemy, because there is unknown land in the crescent north of the Sarmatic Sea as far as the 180th meridian. The eastern side, which is divided by what is known as the Circle, is likewise ringed by unknown territory; and finally, as Ptolemy said in his seventh volume, there was land with islands of a marvellous size from Cattigara up to the promontory Prasum/Prasus.

"Africa is bordered in the middle by strange terrain, so half the length of the whole globe was familiar to him: there are sixty-three degrees from the equator to the north, but to the south Ptolemy knew only seventeen degrees of latitude.

"All the rest is unfamiliar to him—often owing to the carelessness of travellers or the extent of the changes from the other regions of the earth, as he says in Book One, Chapter Five. And when I saw that this had been traversed by modern man and had perhaps been kept secret I could not refrain from taking up my pen to add to that work so that whomsoever might read it and comprehend should praise our efforts and we should thus succeed in making our name eternal as long as that of the great Ptolemy endures.

"We have indicated precisely the relationships of the circles to the world's regions. The ocean is in thin lines and coloured throughout; the coast and the areas around separately; the islands; the satrapies, the most important regions in their own colour and print—all of these are delineated most diligently. Neither have we neglected the rivers, mountains and swamps. Finally we have marked in the latitude known to Ptolemy with the meridian extended down to the Pole. The other two quarters, which one must imagine as being on the far side, have also been added in so that one can see at a glance the whole picture. But I should like to ask of you: do not prejudge anything until you have investigated everything very carefully, so that it becomes more comprehensible.

"Greetings from the scholarly reader Glareanus. From our Aristotelian Academy at Cologne. In the year 1510 of Our Lord's Incarnation as a babe. The 3rd day before/after 1st April." (The dating of the actual day is not done in the traditional way and is thus not entirely clear.)

Glareanus was only twenty-two when he produced this incredible work! He studied literature at Cologne University from 1506, and on March 11th 1510 he gained permission to "strive for the laurels of Doctor". That same year he achieved a distinction in the faculty of "fine arts and philosophy".

The text is a very remarkable one indeed! We can only presume that Glareanus, this young and gifted student of twenty-two, added virtually half the world to a Ptolemaic projection—and with no "copying" involved!

America is included—he uses the names Isabella and Espaniola, so he must have had access to Columbus' voyages—as are Iceland and Greenland. But the most curious fact is the depiction of South America in a form which shows that Glareanus

197

must have known exactly what its shape really was. Further-more, he was aware that it ended in a point and was not joined to Antarctica—and this ten years before Magellan! And the curved shape of the west coast of South America is too good to be accidental. North America is also shown—and that in 1510!

In certain other respects the map shows some inaccuracies such as the size of Africa; but in any event Glareanus is more exact and more detailed than any similar map-maker! Piri Reis and Waldseemüller give only fragmentary parts of the American hemisphere: the young Glareanus achieved the distinction of being the first man to produce an entire map of the New World.

Incidentally the white line you see in the northern part of South America has not been added, but is the result of age: there is a similar line above Java Minor and Major running to the right of the chart.

To sum up: first come Martin Waldseemüller's maps of the New World; then Piri Reis produces his equally strange charts; and finally appears a bombshell from the genius Glareanus! This evidence cannot be dismissed lightly as a matter of chance; it upsets very considerably the ideas most of us hold about this part of our history! And let us not forget the map of the Atlantic islands which was consulted by Columbus two-thirds of the way through his first voyage.

This brings us inevitably to the question of whether Glareanus Piri Reis and Columbus—and indeed even Magellan—made use of a map that already showed parts of the New World? It can hardly be otherwise! Map-making around 1500 was a lengthy and demanding business; besides which one must not forget that before a map can be produced journeys must be made to those regions that are to be mapped! Both South *and* North America must, of necessity, have been discovered and navigated before any map could have been made; and this could not have occurred in the eighteen years between 1492 and 1510. Such journeys often took decades to complete, and even then it would have taken a long time to assemble the material from which Glareanus was able to create his map. And all this would have been at a time when, according to the history books, the golden age of voyages of discovery had only just begun.

We believe that there must have been an older map of America, or at least a detailed description of the regions, which provided the necessary information. How old this map may have been and whether it will ever be found or its creator known remain obscure for the time being. We have seen that cartography was influenced—if not dominated by—the ideas of Ptolemy for a good 1300 years; and this was a very long time indeed, time enough for anything to happen, even the discovery and mapping of America! Nobody today doubts that the Vikings discovered that continent long before Columbus, yet scarcely ten years ago anyone saying as much would have been held to ridicule. Yet now people say that it is quite obvious!

It is a pity that the Glareanus map has suffered so much since 1510—or really since 1482, because that was the year of the original version. There are dozens of names and inscriptions on it, including those in North and South America, but we could not decipher them even with a strong magnifying glass. Scientific aids, such as quartz lamps and X-ray equipment, are needed; the inscriptions will then certainly become legible, and nobody will be amazed if further enigmas are unveiled and other riddles solved. It is now up to the experts: but nevertheless we shall have already placed question-marks against several historic voyages of discovery!

# PART FIVE

# The Ancients

# Chapter Eighteen

The Ancients: the oldest civilization in the world?

Throughout this book the reader will have become aware of our theory that prior to any civilization as yet known to us, another and still older one must have existed; and it is even possible that there was more than one such civilization. Unless we make such an assumption, there is no acceptable explanation of the sudden and simultaneous upsurge of cultures in the ancient world and their diffusion over considerable regions of the world.

In all these civilized centres, man had lived as a *very* simple hunter, farmer or nomad for thousands of years through his ability to avoid death from starvation, with no apparent desire for a higher level of culture; yet all of a sudden, a considerable number of cultures developed almost simultaneously—an amazing concidence, particularly if one remembers their extremely long prehistories. This cannot conceivably be a matter of chance.

Many scientific people—who miss the point—will say that our arguments are "impossible", and will base their own conclusions on the *assumed* differences of date of origin of these various cultures. But we can counter these arguments by claiming that the dates of origin usually given are purely fictional and are anyway extremely vague and indefinite. Furthermore our knowledge of the subject is incomplete, in which respect the whole thing is very much like a jigsaw puzzle: the pieces slowly fit in, but each one alters the picture as it does so. Previously accepted data have to be put aside, and our ideas about these ancient cultures change as a result. But even the severest critics should be satisfied if we say that all the ancient civilizations, except the American ones, developed within, let us say, a thousand years of each other. Leaving aside the "cosmidiotic" theories as of no consequence here, it still is impossible to explain how great civilizations like those of Egypt, China, the Land of Two Rivers, the Indus cultures (Harappa—and Mohenjo-Daro), Crete and other areas could have arisen within this period in view of the enormous distances between them and such natural obstacles as water, deserts and mountains. There is no one clue that would explain this common urge to acquire a higher level of culture: no causes are known for this remarkable communal impetus.

There are some experts who, unable to provide an explanation themselves, support the so-called "mathematical law" of the French philsopher François Meyer, who asserts that any one period of time is five times as quickly traversed as its predecessor: a theory that is based on figures supplied by Unesco on world populations and culture.

We believe this holds true only for recent periods, but certainly not for the old civilizations. After all, modern man has existed for around 30,000 years, and even if we allow 10,000 years, or even longer, for his most primitive stage, this still leaves 20,000 years to be accounted for. According to Meyer's so-called law, the succeeding stages should have lasted 4000 and 800 years respectively. It cannot be a mathematical law, for what is omitted from the calculations is the fact that almost all the ancient cultures have had a lengthy period, or even several periods, of decadence during which the great kingdoms disintegrated and split into numerous small states.

Other people consider the civilization of the Land of Two Rivers to be the "mother-culture", without grasping the consequences of such a theory. This is to assume that the Land of Two Rivers was the source of all the other civilizations of the ancient world; but there are many arguments against this, which make it necessary for us to refer to Egypt and China.

Egypt is one of the most intensively studied of these civilizations, yet we can find no evidence that the source of its civilization lay in the Land of Two Rivers, although we agree that the two cultures influenced each other. The theory seems even more bizarre when applied to China; unfortunately China has not yet been studied in great detail, but we know that its civilization can be traced back to around 3000 B.C. and should therefore, if the theory is correct, have had contacts either by land or sea with the Sumerians of the Tigris and Euphrates. Yet there is nothing to support this assumption.

Numerous other theories have been put forward, varying from the idea that Egypt was the primary source of civilization —which is chronologically impossible—to equally dubious notions about extra-terrestrial civilizations. As for the concept of a "divine spark", it is really too far-fetched.

What we think happened is this: somewhere on earth a civilization arose, or perhaps several such civilizations, which because of extremely favourable conditions flowered earlier than any others. This enabled its people to build up an advantage over all the rest, giving them a clear start of a thousand years or more.

Some of you will ask why, if this civilization had such an advantage, the peoples of other cultures had to wait so long to benefit from it. But this is easily answered: the favoured race, whom for the sake of convenience we call the Ancients, would have felt no urgency about handing over their knowledge to others, for the same reasons as those which persuaded, for example, the Phoenicians and the Carthaginians to take all possible measures to protect their trade. They kept their routes and trading areas secret so that there would always be a shortage of their goods among the peoples with whom they traded. It was only later that the Ancients were forced to help other peoples to develop in order to survive themselves. We believe that one or more natural disasters destroyed this original civilization, and that its survivors found refuge among the inhabitants of those favoured areas which later gave rise to the ancient civilizations we now know about. This is the only theory which virtually meets all the objections and fills even the gaps we are reminded of in old myths and legends!

It may have been a flood, or one of the disasters referred to by the Egyptian priest in his discussions with Solon, which swept away this civilization. Those outside the disaster areas or away trading in other parts of the world managed to survive, and they began to instruct the people among whom they found themselves, on the strength of their higher level of civilization.

Of course much would have depended on the survivors' own degree of skill and those who survived would by no means all have been specialists; which explains at last why the great civilizations were in broad outline much the same and why the differences between them consisted of details only, such as the materials used. We believe that these differences of detail resulted from the varying degrees of skill possessed by the inhabitants. It is not difficult to imagine that an architect or shipbuilder might by chance have reached Egypt, while different specialists settled in the Land of Two Rivers and elsewhere.

Yet despite their differences, they all shared the same inheritance; some may have been more expert than others in particular fields, but all were familiar with the appearance of, for instance, the buildings once erected by the vanished race. Our theory fills another gap here, explaining why buildings found in Egypt, Mesopotamia, the Indus and even China all looked much alike from the outside even though they differed in the materials used and on the inside; a good example being the similarities between Egyptian and Central American pyramids. Although the civilizations of the American Indians were definitely more recent than those of Egypt, Crete, and Mesopotamia, and could not have arisen at the same time, it is quite feasible that the descendants of the Ancients were responsible for the similarities between Maya, Inca and other cultures in the New World and those on this side of the Atlantic. Travel by sea was known thousands of years before our era, and we are slowly beginning to know more about the great seafarers of those times.

It now appears that the Cretans, the Egyptians, the Phoenicians and many others had fleets which were enormous even by today's standards, and that their ships were completely seaworthy. We cannot understand why this fact is not faced and why people are afraid to draw the only logical conclusion: that the ancient sea-going races were not limited to the Mediterranean. We consider it quite possible that one or even several of these races may have discovered America; numerous finds support this theory, although their authenticity is fiercely challenged.

Those who survived the disasters which befell the Ancients brought other and far-reaching consequences to the inhabitants of areas such as Egypt. Although the Ancients must have been largely illiterate, they needed improved communications in the form of writing. Some of those who survived may have completely mastered a form of writing, while others would only have been able to remember some of the symbols used by the Ancients, but both would have contributed towards the formation of a pictorial type of writing. It has been known for a long time that all the ancient scripts are related to one another in some way or another: for instance, Cretan Linear A and B, Old Semitic, Cyprian, the Phoenician alphabet, Hettitic and Goeblitic cuneiform all have many signs in common, and this is to take only a small selection. It seems likely that although these scripts have certain features in common they differed originally as a result of the varying degrees of skill possessed by those few surviving Ancients who had taught them to the local inhabitants. Later on more contact was made between the various civilizations, as a result of which the signs were exchanged and adopted, as a result of which their similarities to each other cannot fail to strike us.

Regrettably there is no space left for us to go deeper into our theories about the Ancients in the present work; there is extensive material to support them, but to elaborate our case in full would need a separate book. Perhaps this is something for the future! But we would like to emphasize yet again that without these theories it is difficult to explain satisfactorily why after living so long in the Stone Ages mankind should have suddenly manifested such a remarkable desire for a higher level of culture; and this is something that cannot be explained as a matter of chance if we bear in mind the time at which it took place, its various locations and the large number of similarities between its different manifestations.

Although our theory about human evolution differs from those of Von Daniken, Charroux and others, we agree with them that something must have been responsible for the simultaneous development of all the ancient civilizations, but beyond this our interpretations differ; while these writers have turned away from the world to find the answer in a "cosmic solution", we have looked for some factor common to all these ancient cultures and originating here on our own planet.

We are convinced that the Ancients existed, and that it will one day be known exactly where they lived; and it is quite possible that when we have discovered this, we will also have resolved the riddle of Atlantis!

# Chapter Nineteen

Conclusions

Where is man heading? This is the question we must try to answer in this last chapter. We said in the introduction that we wanted to help the reader to come to his own conclusions about the problems posed by both our past and our future. This book has been concerned chiefly with the past, but also to some extent with the present and future; and as a result it is virtually impossible to avoid a confrontation with our opponents and their theories—namely those who consider that mankind has been influenced by an extra-terrestrial agency or super-race. Because the question of how the various ancient cultures developed simultaneously has not been solved until now, people have tried to find an answer in the universe, and have looked for evidence of an extra-terrestrial civilization that was responsible for bringing this about. Yet we would like to ask them and their supporters if they are aware of the fact that if there are intelligent beings on remote planets, it is extremely unlikely that they would have anything in common with our own way of life.

We have known for years that there is an almost infinite number of possible circumstances in which the beings of intelligent life could develop; but the form of life need not be like our own in any respect whatsoever as far as structure, behaviour or evolution are concerned. Even hydrogen and oxygen—which are essential to life as we know it—might be lethal to life elsewhere. The following conditions would have to be met in full if a form of life anything like our own were to exist elsewhere in space: the same types of sun and moon as ours with the same mass, rate of revolution and distance from the earth; the planet would similarly need the same mass, composition, gravitational force and atmosphere as earth; and finally the same flora and fauna would be necessary, while the inhabitants would need to be at an identical evolutionary stage to ourselves.

This involves such a large number of factors, each one of which is crucial, that we can safely assume there never was such a planet and never will be.

We do not rule out the possibility of intelligent life existing elsewhere: on the contrary, we *believe* it does! But it is not necessary for such civilizations to be anything like our own. By asking whether a form of life somewhere out in space has ever influenced developments on earth, our opponents transfer attention from the problem of the origin of the ancient civilizations and focus instead on modern sciences like physics and astronomy: the initial problem no longer plays a significant role in their deliberations.

Meanwhile other related subjects also claim their attention. For instance, the UFO question is waiting to be investigated further; in fact the Unidentified Flying Object (or Flying Saucer, as it is popularly known) has become a subject of much public concern, especially in recent years. It is believed that they are not physically present, but manifest themselves temporarily in a visible form. We can see them occasionally but only in a form that exists on another planet and not on our own.

Although our scientists have as yet no idea of how this effect can be achieved, it may be possible for them to do so in the very distant future; and it may also be possible that an extraterrestrial civilization of the kind advocated by our opponents possessed this power. It remains very hard to imagine, since it implies that these creatures can be perceived even though they are not physically present—which would have presented considerable difficulties! If this were the case, how do people imagine that our extra-terrestrial visitors could have taught whole generations of men on earth and carried out other important functions? Actual physical presence would surely have been vital for life and work among those living on earth. But leaving aside this particular problem and assuming that extra-terrestrial beings visited the earth and stayed here for some time, we are then faced with a further problem, namely the unimaginable distances involved. Despite the theory we have just mentioned, our opponents generally believe in the actual physical presence on earth of these extra-terrestrial beings; but can they suggest how the huge distance between our planet and a comparable planet out in space could have been bridged? Proxima Centauri, for instance, which is the nearest star to us of the one thousand million stars of the Milky Way, is a mere 4·3 light years away! Light travelling from Proxima Centauri at a speed of 300,000 kilometres per second takes over four years to reach the earth: that is to say, the distance involved is $4·3 \times 365 \times 24 \times 60 \times 300,000$ km. $= 4·3 \times 9, 463 \times 1012$ km. $= 40$ billion kilometres!

In order to cover that distance in a reasonable time—say forty years—the extra-terrestrial visitors would have needed a space vehicle capable of a speed of 30,000 km. per second. Our modern rockets still need a good hour to cover such a distance, and in order to reach Proxima Centauri within forty years would have to be 3600 times faster than they are at present! And what about the return journey? Such journeys can only be realized in the realms of science fiction—and in the "free time-scale" of certain thinkers.

We are aware that experiments on a very limited scale have begun on propulsion by photon and ion energy sources. The American rocket expert Dr E. Stuhlinger visualizes a spacecraft with a small nuclear reactor inside it. The ions, which can be harnessed without too much loss of mass, can be repelled by a powerful electro-magnetic field; once this process has been set going outside the gravitational field of the earth, the rocket, starting at zero speed in a satellite orbit, should theoretically increase its velocity until the speed of light is finally reached. The photon rocket is supposed to work with the mass/energy Einstein ascribes to light, and it should be possible to utilize the radiation energy of light for propulsion—this could be light which was naturally present or artificial light.

The "plasma rocket" is just as revolutionary, since it could be powered by ionized gases. Although we are slowly getting used to the idea of the impossible becoming possible, these methods of propulsion are as yet little more than ideas; and even if it became possible to approach the speed of light there would still be problems of navigation, reduction of speed when approaching a planet and so forth.

It would also be essential to protect such a spaceship against cosmic rays and meteorites. We know these exist, but as yet we have had no troublesome experiences with them at present-day speeds: however, it would be a different matter in the case of a space vehicle travelling at the velocity of light. Any spaceship dashing through the universe at such a speed without radiation protection or energized defence—which has yet to be invented—would certainly find a collision with cosmic dust or a meteorite fatal.

If in the light of all these problems we were to decide that our space creatures had not arrived from Proxima Centauri, but from somewhere nearer home, like Mars or Venus, we would have to realize that the atmosphere and other conditions in these planets would make it impossible for such extra-terrestrial beings to be like us in any respect whatsoever, since it is well-known that there is a total lack of water, oxygen, warmth and atmosphere on these planets. This of course does not preclude the possibility of life existing under completely different conditions, though it does raise the question of how such beings could have lived on earth for generations under conditions that would be lethal to them.

The planets of our solar system can therefore be rejected; yet our opponents still insist that these visitors were physically present on earth, in which case we still have to face the problem of the enormous distances involved; and it should be remembered that we took our neighbouring star, Proxima Centauri, as our example, rather than the Andromeda formation, the dimensions of which are comparable to our own solar system—and which is about 2,000,000 light years away!

There is another point worth bearing in mind: what value would such a meeting have had for the extra-terrestrial civilization? Let us visualize the situation: cosmonauts of a superior race from out in space, highly intelligent and skilled beings, come face to face on one of their stellar or interstellar journeys with Stone Age man who scarcely knows anything about farming, writing and so on and is not even able to communicate with his fellow men in remote places!

It is unrealistic for us to consider ourselves the centre of the universe, particularly at the present time! And nothing has really changed for the better from prehistoric times to the present-day! A super-civilization from outer space would surely have avoided contact with the "lords of creation"—and may have tried to prevent us from launching out into space.

The only aspect of man's life which has actually changed over the millennia is the technological one, which has developed enormously: we are now able to exterminate our fellow men— or persuade them to accept our ways of thinking—with hideous weapons, very different from the axes, spears and clubs of yesterday. Even as you read this, people are being killed all over the world and others are being allowed to die of hunger in spite of all our prosperity; on top of which we seem to be incapable of looking after the air we breathe, the food we eat and the water we drink.

Taking these facts into account, it must be very unlikely that any race from beyond our planet would have run the risk of contact with us and with the Augean stables we have created for ourselves; and this may explain why the UFOs remain "intangible", since—if they exist—they too would try to avoid all contact with mankind!

All these arguments can be summarized in one sensible question: why should so much ingenuity go into elaborating theories that are beyond the range of our imagination and quite remote from the reality of our lives when we have here on earth, within the bounds of feasibility, another explanation of the origins of the early civilizations? We are, of course, referring to our theory about the Ancients.

There is only one obstacle in the way of this theory, which is that scholars have not yet found any evidence which satisfies *them* as to the existence of such a central culture, as a result of which they reject our ideas: we cannot regret this, because otherwise we would have had no reason for writing this book. Scholars have always reacted like this, especially those who claim to have a monopoly of the truth; we have our being in the struggle between what must come and what will not go away.

It may be that you prefer our opponents' extra-terrestrial theories, not just because they defend a point of view which has more appeal than our more earthbound one, but also because they fall back on a mysterious yet cut-and-dried solution, as a result of which you do not have to lose a night's sleep. That is a perfectly understandable reaction—just as understandable as that of the ostrich which puts its head in the sand when danger threatens, and just as natural as that of someone in today's society who turns to drugs, marijuana or alcohol to flee from a world bent on self-destruction in which man no longer belongs.

If that is your reaction, then there is plenty of reading matter here for you; but it still leaves us with the question—*Homo sapiens, quo vadis?*

# Index

# Index

219

# Sources of the photos